Contents

Volume 96:2 Summer 2006

Poems

Centrefold

Reviews

Endpapers

POEMS

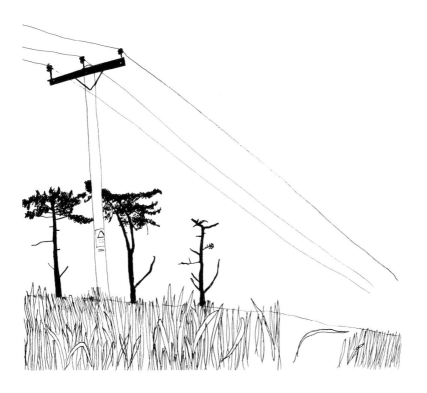

...beasts and angels
simmering like rain against the skin...
—John Burnside

Don Paterson
Two Versions From
Rilke's *Sonnets to Orpheus*:
Change

The world can no more keep its form
than clouds can in the sky;
yet all perfected things fall home
to their antiquity.

Above the changing and the dead,
freer, wider, higher –
your first song still rings on ahead,
O god with the lyre.

Our pain still comes as a surprise;
our love has not been learned;
the very reason for our death

stays wholly undiscerned.
Only the song above the Earth
hallows and glorifies.

The Double Realm

Does he belong here? No, his spacious nature
had its birth in both realms. Who has dwelt
among the willow's roots will weave the osier
so much more deftly in the upper light.

When you blow the candle out, don't leave the bread
or milk still on the table, for the shades
are drawn by them. But he can *raise* the dead,
and conjured through his half-transparent lids

confuses their dark land in everything:
the lore of earth-smoke, meadow-rue and may
appear as real to him as their bright bloom.

Nothing can diminish the true emblem.
Whether lifted from the hearth or the cold clay,
let him praise the pitcher, torque and ring.

John Burnside
from Responses To Augustine Of Hippo:
Retractationes

If, as he says,
the flaw in the weft of the soul

is how it tends, forever,
towards nothingness,

then might we not imagine it
as grace itself,

the way it teeters,
this side of extinction,

locked with a flesh
that is possibly not, after all,

as loathsome as he thought,
but just as much

illumined, steady,
pitched just at the point

where everything might stop,
and nothing happens;

　　*

and how it resembles love is the way
it might be the last occasion, sitting alone
in the kitchen, as dusk filters in:

how any moment now, the known might end,
or end for me, at least, while, somewhere else,
someone is cooking a meal, or writing a letter.

Out in the garden, the shadows merge with the dark,
till all I have taken for granted – the half-truths of form,
the goodwill of definition –

is folded up, as matter always is,
falling away, like the undelivered soul,
toward nothingness.

As a child, I imagined the silence of the dead
was the silence of disapproval;
or else, a mild distaste for how I went on

living, not quite sure of shapes and colours.
Later, it seemed they had stumbled upon a world
so innocent of names, the whole event

was one enormous household, beasts and angels
simmering like rain against the skin,
as if the soul were not the uttered word,

as if the colours were those perfect forms
he always wanted, blithe, Platonic blues
and reds, and not the accidents of light

that shift and flicker in the fading lawn,
the dimming fire amidst the Deutzia,
antirrhinums, milkweed, evening primrose.

Yet surely the dead are soulless, not being here,
where souls are made,
in shadows and greening leaves:

soulless, and poised at the rim
of chaos, they long to return,
to sit up alone all night, in kitchens like this,

remembering,
forgetting,
being lost.

As a child I imagined the life beyond this life
as one enormous room, all
mist and kinship,

now I would have to insist on walls and factions,
hidden compartments, corridors leading off
to secret gardens steeped in changing light,

not to be set apart, but to meet again
in the old way, coming together
by chance, on an aimless walk

through foxgloves, or Michaelmas daisies,
losing and winning back
the sense of the other,

sun on a stranger's skin, and that quickening
when someone else is there,
as yet unseen:

    *

and it isn't a choice I would make,
to rise again,

but somewhere between
this one life and the next

I imagine a point
where the soul

is purified:
fogged water leaching through spawn

and the veins
of cowslips;

and this just another event
like an egg, or a sunrise,

a sense of someone waking in the dark
and dressing by a window, looking out

at stars, from time to time, a neighbour's tree,
a sound in the distance like love, or a passing train,

as he teases a bone into place
or straightens a nerve,

preparing to happen again,
in a knowable world,

though all the while puzzled
by something he ought to remember.

W. S. Merwin
Empty Lot

There was only the narrow alley between us
and we lived every day next to the long dusty patch
of high ragweed that first parched summer
and then the heart leaves of the old poplar cradled
down to the dust in the fall when men gathered there
of an evening to toss quoits into the sky
toward the clay pits facing them and in winter
the drifted snow showed where the wind swooped whirling
between the houses and I watched the sun go down
out beyond there behind the mountain
and the moon sailing over the lot late at night
when I woke out of a dream of flying
and yet there was no way to imagine that place
as it had been for so long when it had
the world to itself before there were houses
when bears took their time there under trees they knew
now we were told that it belonged to
the D & H Coal Company who
would not do anything with it but keep it
in case they ever should need to sink
an emergency shaft to miners
in trouble below there nobody could say
how far down but sometimes when the night
was utterly still we knew we had just heard
the muffled thump of a blast under us
and the house knew it the windows trembled and we
waited listening for picks ticking in the dark

Europe

After days untold the word
came You will see it
tomorrow you will
see what you have only heard of
ever since you were too small
to understand and that night
which I would scarcely remember
I lay looking up through
the throb of iron at sea
trying again to remember
how I believed it would look
and in the morning light
from the bow of the freighter
that I know must have gone by now
to the breaker's decades ago
then I could make out the shadow
on the horizon before us
that was the coast of Spain
and as we came closer another
low shape passing before it
like a hand on a dial
a warship I recognised
from a model of it I had made
when I was a child and beyond it
there was a road down the cliff
that I would descend some years later
knowing it when I reached it
there they were all together
it seemed for the first time

Escape Artist

When they arrange the cages
for experiments
they have long known
that there is no magic
in foxes at any time
singly or by species
colour region gender
whether in the wild
or after generations
bred in captivity
for some grade of fur
or trait of character
for the benefit
of a distant
inquiring relative
living in ambush and hope
in clothes and mourning

but what after all
was magic and where
could it have come from
as the experts considered this
wordless descendant
of countless visions
apparitions tales
that vanished in the telling
this heir of conjurors
of disappearing acts
caged now in numbers
lost in pain sight

Jacob Polley
The Owls

I hear the owls in the dark yews
behind the house – children out late
or lost, their voices worn away.
They've forgotten their names and wait

to be called again by mothers
who miss them, so they might return
with fingers and human faces.
But their sadness, too, is long gone.

Their voices are as empty
and unlovable as glass
and no one calls into the trees.

Little gods, they've forsaken us
as we have them! They sit and cry,
glorified, and couldn't care less.

Brew

I'm stewing your tea. Can't you see
my heart's steeped in it, honey?
As I wind honey round a spoon
to sweeten it, doesn't this prove
I even hold your sweet tooth dear
among all your teeth? Is it clear?
I stir in milk and the world turns
in your teacup. My stomach churns.
You warm your hands on the cup: see
how it breathes, how you throttle me?
Though the obsolete clock still ticks
I measure my time, sip by sip.
Is it hot, strong, and sweet enough?
Say it's all three. Say it'll do.
Say you like something in it
but you're not sure what: I'll know.
Say when you're finished we're not
and don't go.

Anna T. Szabó
She Leaves Me

She betrays me, she leaves me.
She pushes me out of herself, and leaves me.
She offers herself to feed on, and leaves me.
She rocks me and she leaves me.
Wipes my bottom, combs my hair,
caresses the soles of my feet, but leaves me.
My nose drinks in her fragrance, how she hugs me:
she says, 'I'll never leave you!' And she leaves me.
She tricks me: smiling, whispers 'Don't be scared!'
I *am* scared, and I'm cold, and yet she leaves me.
She lies down on the bed with me at evening,
but soon enough she slips away and leaves me.
She is so big, so warm, alive, a nest,
she kisses me, and hums to me, and leaves me.
She presses sweets into my open palms
and 'There you are, eat now,' she says, and leaves me.
I cry and howl and press her frame to mine;
I can hold her, hit her too; and yet she leaves me.
She shuts the door, does not look back at all,
I'm nothing when she leaves me.
I wait for her return, a cringing cur:
she then arrives and strokes me, and she leaves me.
I need her – it is death to live without her –
she picks me up to warm me, and she leaves me.
Her arms make up a cage, her lap's a house;
I'd love to go back in there, but she leaves me.
I come to one conclusion: I'm not her:
a stranger, she's a stranger, and she leaves me.

Out there's the world, where someone will be waiting!
For you, there will be someone there to leave.
Don't look back. Shut the door. You know
how easy it is to wait, how hard to go.
Some you'll grieve, others will deceive you,
some will wait, others fear your lack,
and some there'll always be who don't come back:
they give you life, but then they die and leave you.

THE BRITISH AND IRISH
CONTEMPORARY POETRY
CONFERENCE 2006

THE LINE OF CONTEMPORARY POETRY
22-24 SEPTEMBER
Hosted by St Anne's College, Oxford, in assocation
with the University of St Andrews, Queen's
University Belfast and Lancaster University

PUBLIC EVENTS IN OXFORD
A limited number of tickets will be available to non-
delegates for these events. Early booking is advised

Saturday 23 September

- **3pm**   The Michael Donaghy Lecture
          Professor Jonathan Bate speaking on
          'The Green Line' of poetry and ecology

- **8pm**   Poetry reading by Kathleen Jamie,
          Michael Longley and Glyn Maxwell

Prices: £6 per event
or £10 for both events

Please send a cheque made
out to BICPC, **including your
email address and a SAE**, to:
BICPC Coordinator,
PO Box 8705,
Nottingham, NG2 9BU

Venue:
St Anne's College, Oxford.
Full details will be
sent out with tickets

ARTS COUNCIL ENGLAND

enquiries: **coordinator@poetryconference.org.uk**   **www.poetryconference.org.uk**

Hospital Window

The now. The melody of moments.
Exterior and interior voices.
The cool whisper of leaves at night.
Autumnal. Branch-flute. Leaf sighs.

Winds flutter. A bite of sky.
Mist. Dark damp. Bars of light.
Great birds, matted wings spread wide.
Ploughland clods. Sun in a void.

A beating pulse. Bones. Nerves.
Hollows deep as wells. Caves.
Roofs. Windows. House-walls.
Echo-emptiness. Cellar smells.

And yet desire for being, being...

The now. The out. The in. The nothing.

Translated by Clive Wilmer and George Gömöri

C. K. Williams
Shrapnel

1.

Seven-hundred tons per inch, I read, is the force in a bomb or shell in the
    microsecond after its detonation,
and two-thousand feet per second is the speed at which the shrapnel, the
    materials with which the ordnance
is packed, plus its burst steel casing, "stretched, thinned, and sharpened" by
    the tremendous heat and energy,
are propelled outwards in an arc until they strike an object and either
    ricochet or become embedded in it.

In the case of insufficiently resistant materials, the shards of shrapnel can
    cause "significant damage";
in human tissue, for instance, rupturing flesh and blood vessels and
    shattering and splintering bone.
Should no essential organs be involved, the trauma may be termed
    "superficial," as by the chief nurse,
a nun, in Ian McEwan's *Atonement*, part of which takes place in a hospital
    receiving wounded from Dunkirk.

It's what she says when a soldier cries, "*Fuck!*" as her apprentice, the
    heroine, a young writer-to-be,
probes a wound with her forceps to extract one of many jagged fragments
    of metal from a soldier's legs.
"Fuck!" was not to be countenanced back then. "How dare you speak that
    way?" scolds the imperious sister,
"Your injuries are superficial, so consider yourself lucky and show some
    courage worthy of your uniform."

The man stays still after that, though "he sweated and... his knuckles turned
    white round the iron bedhead."
"Only seven to go," the inexperienced nurse chirps, but the largest chunk,
    which she's saved for last, resists;
at one point it catches, protruding from the flesh – ("He bucked on the bed
    and hissed through his teeth") –
and not until her third resolute tug does the whole "gory, four-inch stiletto
    of irregular steel" come clear.

2.

"Shrapnel throughout the body," is how a ten-year old killed in a recent
    artillery offensive is described.
"Shrapnel throughout the body:" the phrase is repeated along with the
    name of each deceased child
in the bulletin released as propaganda by our adversaries, at whose
    operatives the barrage was directed.
There are photos as well – one shows a father rushing through the street,
    his face torn with a last frantic hope,

his son in his arms, rag-limp, chest and abdomen speckled with deep, dark
    gashes and smears of blood.
Propaganda's function, of course, is exaggeration: the facts are there,
    though, the child is there... or not there.
...As the shrapnel is no longer there in the leg of the soldier: the girl holds
    it up for him to see, the man quips,
"Run him under the tap, Nurse, I'll take him home," then, "...he turned to
    the pillow and began to sob."

Technically, I read, what's been called shrapnel here would have once been
    defined as "splinters" or "fragments."
"Shrapnel" referred then only to a spherical shell, named after its inventor,
    Lieutenant Henry Shrapnel.
First used in 1804, it was "...guaranteed to cause heavy casualties... the best
    mankiller the army possessed."
Shrapnel was later awarded a generous stipend in recognition of his
    contribution "to the state of the art."

Where was I? The nun, the nurse; the nurse leaves the room, throws up; the
fictional soldier, the real child...

The father... What becomes of the father? He skids from the screen, from
the page, from the mind...

Shrapnel's device was superseded by higher-powered, more efficient
projectiles, obsolete now in their turn.

One war passes into the next. One wound is the next and the next.
Something howls. Something cries.

Lucien Jenkins
Kick Away

A long way after Michel Deguy's Qui Quoi

A long time ago this world was begun
        and you did not exist
your face is on every poster   my train
        pauses to let the fast

intercity service whiz by   I have
        sinned   sins of omission
commission   emission   the purple mushrooms
        on that balcony

while the dog barked   do you remember the smell
        of the sea   my mouth's fears
have been punished since   filled with fraying
        questions   vain tears.

Bill Manhire
Quebec

The café was called Quebec. We used to go there a lot.

The first time, well, we simply liked the name. They had nothing local, but you could ask for anything else.

In winter they served up hot, brutal stews, which we ate like soup, using a spoon, and there were rough slabs of some home-made nutty bread. It was all new to us. In summer, the desserts were airy, filled with berry fruit, or made with lemon.

Before it was Quebec, it was Kerouac's. Before that, I think it was Fettucine, and before that it was a bookshop, Tom's Exchange. The man who ran it wore a grey dustcoat; he wasn't Tom. Tom was never there.

This was years before we met. As I recall, the days were long and awkward. You could take in a few coins and a couple of old paperbacks, and come back out with something you hoped might change your life.

Frolic

late at night the lake grows just
a little more laconic
like it wants not to want

to say something

+

moonlight (she says)

like flower, like
lick of water

like le lac

+

& then the managed river drops away

The Workshop

I tick the death of Angela's father.
I query the way Fitch fell in love.
Ken has too many sisters; maybe he needs a stronger mother.
Craft, we say. Life. How can we make this better?

Andrew Motion
Last Things

I locked my door and went for nothing much –
Just supermarket stuff, the usual –
But felt at once how things I'd left behind
Rejoiced to see me go, and be themselves:
A knife-blade shivered at a fork's cold touch,
Two cushions reddened on each other's swell,
A book sprang open, riffled, then explained
The reasons it preferred life off the shelf.

And in the bedroom, tweaking from the bed
To make a taut, free-floating trampoline,
The sheet rose up and hovered in mid-air,
So everything about me that was dead
Already – hair, and flakes of withered skin –
Could bounce, and dance, until I reappear.

Conversation:
Aboard

Anthony Thwaite
Sententia

Somewhere above the Norwegian Sea
At thirty-thousand feet or thereabouts,
The outside air unimaginably cold,
A woman sits and knits with needles poised
Above a cup of water, and it sways.

What this suggests is strange. Our restless days
Are put in order, regulated, praised
When even some small skill can grip and hold
The chaos and the danger and the doubts
That float above, below, continually.

Sarah Wardle
Found Audience

Faced with this train carriage, you want to recite to them,
lines of how the sunlight hits their office windowsills
just so, the concert of traffic below, discourses
of computer programmes and their accounts team,
the walk of the woman they desire, the man they conjure

by the vending machine. You want to speak
when you walk through London streets of the temples
that were here before the skyline spires, of the river
before it knew its name, of the land before people,
its primeval blood and mire. You want to listen

to daylight filtered through leaves, the stone of the city,
the dust of the place. You want to hear the voices
of those who worked here before you now, and left no trace.
You circle over familiar ground. Wherever you travel,
you reach a starting point, the beginning of ending.

You're an unreeled thread, spinning through weekdays
till the wheel's upright. Watch how these feet could belong
to another, as you walk the race-course of the platform's length
and return to the starting gates, the ticket barrier to thought,
and pass through like a battery egg. The day's under

starter's orders and you're off in a world of dream-making
to the power of ten. You shoot down the escalator,
as if it's a playground slide, into the tunnel of ghost frowns.
The platform's three deep. The train's late. Silence
expands to fill the lack of space. You badly need

to read *Four Quartets* or *The Sonnets to Orpheus*
in each person's face. But here, before the London terminus,
you want to say only that ringed dates draw nearer
like six o'clock departure, or these trees now
speeding into lost distance, becoming the green future

we'll drive at this evening under purple skies, preparing
for another sleep, the pentameter of the rail ever broken in half
by the caesura of a change of track, the way the echo answers
back, as heads loll and they are lulled by rhythmic comfort,
catching up on missed life. You want to tell them that.

Daljit Nagra
Yobbos!

The first step towards lightening THE WHITE MAN'S burden is through
teaching the virtues of cleanliness.
– Pears Soap, from advert, 1899

A right savage I was – sozzled
to the nose with sprightly
Muldoon, squeezed into the communal

sweat of a Saturday tube home –
I'm up to p388 of his sharp lemon-skinned
Collected Poems

when some scruffy looking git pipes to his crew –
some Paki shit, like,
eee's loookin into!

My blood rising, especially when my head's
done in with words like
'Badhbh'... 'Cailidin'... 'Salah-eh-din',

I nearly get blunt, as one of them –
well mate, this Paki's more British than that inde-
cipherable, impossibly untranslatable

sod of a Paddy –
only I don't 'cos I catch my throat gungeing
on its Cromwellian vile, my tongue foaming for soap...

Tamar Yoseloff
Voyage

The train sails through fields, docks in middle-
manager cities: Coventry, Milton Keynes,
the track before us a fact of our expansion,
the night inevitable – sick phosphorescence of lights
coming on, of platforms rushing past,
the names of towns illegible with speed,
their tower blocks blown back in a sudden squall.
On the page a man is drowning:
I only have to close the book to forget him.
He's history. The present is about the train
hurtling past on the opposite track, steering
for where I've just been; the flotsam of travel:
the paper cup, the empty miniature,
the folded tabloid. Old news. Salt on my tongue.

Tomaž Šalamun
White Hash, Black Weed, Gregor Is Telling Me What You Are Doing

In the chalk of a white blur humour is
stuffed. People keep asking me how I
dip my eyelids. The simplest thing:

the skin, you caress the dolphin, sometimes
you burn Armenia. Diran understands
exactly. Hash helps, hash is a walker.

Not for him, he's black, weed is for him.
Marco called again. He really wants to buy
Lindos. And I think about Juan (his mother-in-law,

a psychiatrist, trained by Lacan, disappointed
by not having enough real customers in Naples)
obviously he gets detached thinking of the Nazca

Lines. They all went away to pick mushrooms,
I'm staying. I dance on yesterday's weed, Diran
types too. He's in the Tower. He has everything

in his computer, but me, if I physically don't cut
wood I get torpid. My cornea gets eaten by
torches, dwarfs in togae roll from geoglyphs.

It hums and if anyone really thought out how
to build a house, that's Juan. In Pittsburgh too
they want me for a semester. Liliana Ursu wants me

to write an introduction for her book. I'm hot in
Kuala Lumpur. Quite known in Singapore. In
Jakarta only within a small circle, but they're

afire. In Jakarta people don't have a lot of
money, they have to borrow my books.
I still have that leaflet, Andrej, you gave me

when we crossed Asia. Everything stored.
I don't invent. I don't lie. I don't exaggerate.
Except when I admire Marco's boat.

A terrible one. It swallows tons of gas.
Of course you can't sell it to anyone else
except a Saudi prince, maybe that one

there in Greece. We did a lot of staring
at each other. Marco designed and
traced it out himself. The invention,

you trace it like a hunting dog. And
we were melancholy everywhere.
In fact, I traced Archilochus.

"Gladstone was a pig. I only liked
Disraeli" I hear clearly. As Pogorelić
got everything from Liszt, everything

from the living, me too, I can now
drink deep into the British Crown.
Strategically it's important. Marco Canoni.

You should check him out. O your eyes,
Queen Victoria. O your white feathers.
The young dots do the same. They're

on the dense, on the tiny and the fresh.
I'm on the rare, on the horrible and the mad.
But not sold out. Not sold out. I'm fighting

with Primoz Kožak's prediction that I will
end as a gilt layer. I only play. Mineral water caresses
my head. Mineral water decides about my loot.

Translated by Joshua Beckman and the author

Tracy Ryan
Softfall

1. Grasp

Second-guesser, forestaller, laying my life's cloak out
in a useless gesture for your small feet to step over;

spinner, wrenching protective gossamer
from her own inner fibre, a barrier

of sorts and in certain dimensions, as if I could ache
with permanent milk and that proved anything

after weaning, a coating, a buffer, edge-beveller,
   rug-straightener,
fool-proofer, airbrusher, mind extending

a feeler, ahead of you, ontological
recapitulator, faithful retainer, overprogrammed

incubator, K-selected,
non-relinquisher. And yet

you grow bigger –
I weed each drawer as your frame

escapes me, replenishing.
I never keep up.

2. Gravity

Watching you fall in the same way twice is
a lesson on the limits of
language –

speechless, I only cradle your head and try
sounding it, depthless, with binary options like
does it hurt a *little* or a *lot?* — and so far you're
too truthful to choose what will please.

Still I go on, issuing words like so much
netting, or wadding, that will eventually, the theory goes,
come in some stable way between you and the
hard ground.

3. Amphibian

After a bath, slippery pup, tadpole, you love to
torment me, as you think, by hiding
face under towel — *Say,*
Where's my little boy? Where is he? Where can he be?

in your ecstasy often forgetting
the punchline, the self-revelation.

You would lie there for hours
kicking those new frog-legs,
naked and cold, but for the veiled face,
if I didn't curtail this.

4. "To Earthward"

The way you crave
to meet the dirt, lock horns with it,
head-butting,
birth-urge in the wrong direction,
or diving as if you took land
for water. Even when burrowing into
your father on the sofa, you call it
the cave, his body
half the world's body, future to
your own. First day

in the new sandpit, you stuff
your mouth with it, grinding
white teeth on white grit, your joy
hysterical — nothing I do
can wean you off it. *Munch on, crunch on*
you keep yelling, unwitting
in your quotation
from the *Pied Piper*
of Hamelin.

5. Bruiser

I watch each one in turn
on your forehead
change size and colour

as if
predicting weather

part science, part superstition,
the repetition

of old wisdom. *It will blow over.*
I make you face the sun,
then turn, to check dilation.

But you look past me, mere
bystander, tender with ice-pack,
cold flannel, soft restricting
limbs, sad ballast

you want no part in:
I'm all right, Mum.

Softfall is the Australian term for soft-landing surfaces in playgrounds.

Friedrich Hölderlin
The Half Of Life

With yellow pears
And full with wild roses
The land hangs into the lake,
You gracious swans
Drunk with kissing
You dip your heads
Into holy-sobering water.

Woe me, where shall I take
The flowers from in winter,
And where the sunshine,
And shadows of earth?
The walls are standing
Speechless and cold, the flags
Jangle in the wind.

Translated by Lotte Kramer

Matthew Sweeney
The Mission

Hiding in the wolfhound's kennel,
hoping the big brute won't return,
he takes the tiny photo out again.
Such a pretty face to make a hole in,
such sad eyes without a reason –
yet... Unless she's always known,
the way dogs know, and disappear
deep into the woods to die alone.
If only she would do the same.
He turns the photo upside down
till her nose sticks up in the U
of her hair, and beneath it
the place he must focus on.
Righted again, there's less of a smile
on those lips, but still a ghost of one.
The face is the face of a battler –
he hopes she's not a gun woman.
He hopes her hound won't save her
by tearing off his face. At that
he hears a car crunch over pebbles.
He replaces the photo in his wallet,
frees his revolver from its holster,
inches his way to the cold air,
whispering her name over and over.

Todd Swift
The Soviet Women Pilots Of WWII –
The Night Witches –

One night flew 18 sorties – willingly attracting enemy fire –
Wingwoman Ryobova and Nadya Popova – "At night

Sometimes I look up into" – lit with danger – Katya
Co-pilot – (*Women Aloft*, Time Life, 1981) – steel to be

A decoy – as Nadya said, "It worked" – it took nerves of –
Confidently stating that, "War requires the ability to kill."

This found poem is based on material discovered on the internet.

George Szirtes
Snowfield

1.
Snow takes form: the shapes it makes mount up
and vanish against sky, a paler more transcendent
cloud, a broader emptiness, briefly dependent
on whatever it clings to, fit for the hands to cup
and pack solid. The quiet solidifies
into a firmer block of silence that shuts
off streets and gardens. Stillness. No wind cuts
our faces. We listen out for whispers and sighs
in the furniture but it is little enough
this light layer: it doesn't change the state
of the world or even Norfolk very much,
only appearances and the curious stuff
of illusion we require to operate
things that we thought were clear and ours to touch.

2.
The *One Stop Shop* stays open. The stationer
and gift shop, the butcher, the winebar, the pub:
commerce happens. Money, white goods and grub,
hygiene products, light fittings, the pensioner
at the Post Office window. Cold fingers at tills,
on the counter, in the pocket. We are a scene
from a Dutch painting moving against a screen
of well-worn properties: frozen ponds, windmills,
spires and barns. Our rural sports are gazing
and passing water. We are our own TV.
Children are born, we listen to their bones
growing, watch hair sprout. They move at amazing
speed through slow-motion air. Our brevity
is startling. We're outlived by trees and stones.

3.

Brief snow. It sits on the roof as though it had
always been there and always will be. It seems
permanent in its grave weirdness. There are reams
of it to be read in invisible ink. It makes sad
comical entertainment discovering its history
of anecdotes, like an elaborate joke that is told
over and over again. The dead and the old
know it by heart as does the snow-covered tree
in the flat field. As do I myself, or I think
I am starting to learn it: that snow is beautiful,
that it settles on us like a hand that is raised
sooner rather than later, that we can sink
into it as into a frozen bath, that each petal
of its crystal flower is lethal and perfectly phrased.

Moniza Alvi
Red Apples

After sleep has escaped you
night after night
someone will say that you look very well.

It's because your cheeks glow
like red apples

from Samuel Palmer's visionary tree.

They're so good, so deceptively good
it's a pity
you can't reach up to your face
and pluck them.

Like the queen in Snow White,
offer them with a smile.

Tiffany Atkinson
In This One

he comes from the garden wearing
nothing but an armful of swiss chard.
His hair curls to the collarbone, and he
has earrings in, for something with each
movement quips back light. And not
a slight man, no. A planetary type. His
skin has sun in its unconscious, not like
mine. He's whistling, bright and abstract.
I am certain he is not from hereabouts.

Of course, I have no garden. Still,
a vase of lilies streaks the air with scent
like spilt milk. And he's all for conversation.
Though my tongue's a husband in a dress-
shop, he does not mind. I could like him,
as it goes. And he could mix a margarita
blindfold. Once he asks, what were you up
to, when I found you here that morning?
I was only writing. Look. A likely story.

Philip Gross
Translucence

A drip of wax, spilled on the white
    spread linen: there's a mystery
    I dwelt on while the grown-ups talked.
Lift it up, just enough: an under-light

inhered in what was stain, and shade
    in white around it – *via negativa*
    for beginners in a tear-splash spot
that was almost a spy hole, contact made

with a close world unknown as next door.
    The wax was, somehow, soft *and* brittle:
    it rucked, then crinkled to the touch,
like silk decayed, the wedding dress I saw

in its museum case (how small had she been,
    the dead bride?) so the thin light held
    inside the fabric was a body, immaterial,
and filled it, like the chamber of the queen

of a smoked-out beehive: a honey-rot smell
    with charring, wax and wing-dust:
    something most there by not being,
like an echo, like an echo in a well.

Susan Taylor
Milkflower

for Rose Flint

She doesn't cut a single stalk to bring these bunches to us.
She reads. Her voice calls us inside a wood and we see
her shadow rise up from her body,

tall and separate; suggestion of Persephone
– always moving, sewing snowdrops

among small crowns of leaves,
patch by patch,
within the dark and slippery contract of a kiss.

Rose, go on
weaving the wet path.

I take from you this poem
for the time of year my farmer-mother calls the Quarter Day
of Candlemas, when spring begins.

My mother loves the way the evening moves, extending
light, as February comes

where once she watched her daughter walk
on her shadow and the snowdrops bend

and multiply
chill pale bells.

Summer Spotlight:
The Francophone Caribbean

This August the oldest poetry festival in Europe, the forty-five-year-old Struga Poetry Evenings, celebrates Caribbean poetry. Struga, a lakeside fishing village on the Albanian-Macedonian border, will host an evening of Caribbean poetry and launch the first Slav-language anthology of writing from the region. The festival's laureate – following in the footsteps of Neruda, Hughes and, recently, Tranströmer and Merwin – will be the Cuban Nancy Moréjon.

Poetry Review is glad to be part of this project; which not only enriches the literary canon in the Balkans, the Caucuses and Central Europe, but sets poets of whom Anglophone readers may be aware in a wider regional context of writing in French and Spanish. Here we feature a small selection of Francophone writing from the anthology. Césaire, forefather of Negritude, and the three middle-generation poets gathered here – Monchoachi, Rippon and Rupaire – bear witness to a poetry which, decade by decade, has helped form regional, cultural and ethnic identities… in ways after all not dissimilar to that of the Balkans.

Max Rippon (b. 1944, Marie-Galante)
Blues Time

Sometimes only you know how
desperately I want to speak on the phone
how nothing keeps going
and the calm water of the mountain-gullies
runs the wrong way

Sometimes you know
I wish nothing had happened
and I could to go to Grand-Bourg
lips closed mouth sewn tight
keeping an eye on your precarious health

Other times again
I want to throw tears on the ground

and tell how I live with profound grief
at knowing you're lying
under the too-heavy load
of the clay of the last journey

Sometimes
when you can see the fragile branch of the kanifis bush
thrashing wildly,
passionate attacks
on the rough bark of the gayak tree,
I put a crutch under my grief.
Then a friend comes –
strong arms
hoped-for help.
We swallow back the ill-fitting
harsh edges of bitter tears
as if to say
nothing's changed here
even if since you went to God
home has let its arms fall,
ashamed displaced
distorted dried-out
at a low ebb…

Often
I want to give you a ring
to say
        everything's going fine
        I've just lost my voice
but you no longer have a number
so
I look up
at the slow, wayward tricks
of milky clouds
to see whether one day,
one single little day in a night of days,
I could meet you again,
your hair in a bun,
at your azure *prie-Dieu.*

From *Rékot: Brisures de mots* 1996

Aimé Césaire (b. 1913, Martinique)
Tam-tam II

For Wifredo

Little steps caterpillar rain
little steps with a mouthful of milk
little steps of ball-bearings
little steps seismic shakes
the yams in the sun pacing with giant steps the spaces of stars
the spaces of the Holy
Mother of God
with giant steps the spaces of words in a throat
of the stuttering
orgasm of holy dirt
Alleluia

From *Les armes miraculeuses 1941*

Rain Blues

Aguacero
fine musician
at the foot of a bare tree
between lost chords
near our worn-out memories
between our worn-out hands
and the people of a foreign power
we leave our eyes hanging
and born
unclasping the bridle of a grief
we weep

From *Cadastre* 1961

Word

          In-between me
and myself,
beyond every star-system,
in my squeezed-shut hands only
the odd gasp of final fever-spasm,
throbs the word
                    I'd have been luckier outside this labyrinth.
Longer larger it throbs
in stronger and stronger waves
in the lasso catching me
in the rope hanging me
all the arrows nailing me
with their bitter poison
to the beautiful axis of utterly fresh stars.

It throbs
the very essence of shadow throbs
in wing in throat risking death
the black word
coming out fully-armed from the yell
of a poisonous flower
the black word
all lousy with parasites
the black word
full of traffickers
grieving mothers
crying children
the black word
a sizzling of flesh that burns
acrid and leathery
the black word
like the sun which bleeds from the claw
on the pavement of clouds
the black world
like the last laugh born out of innocence
between the tiger's fangs

and as the word sun is a smacking of bullets
and as the word night's a taffeta you rip
the black word
                        is heavy you know
with the thunder of a summer
            which takes
                        incredible liberties.

From *Corps perdu* 1949

But There's This Wrong

If my thought borrows fish-hawk wings
be sure
you're prey to my talons

                        as I am
to the beak of wind of doubt of soot
of cinder-night thickening towards the heart
and this stuttering of nails which beat against the seasons.

Because there's this wrong
telling lies on the pinnacle of myself,
a spring without ripples hidden in a great pool,
when ravenous day picks up my scent

you'll say this blood of mine
always reins-in its bitter gallop at the brink,
that my lie's fairer before God than their
accurate mouths:

before His helpless face a thousand children will rise
from the high sea diving up on the bare bulkhead
roused from the original black sob of thorns.

From *Ferrements* 1960

Lagoon Calendar

I live in a sacred wound
I live in ancestors of the imagination
I live in an obscure want
I live in a long silence
I live in an irredeemable thirst
I live in a thousand-year journey
I live in a three-hundred-year war
I live in a deconsecrated faith between bulb and corm
I live in an unexploited space
I live in a basalt *No*, a flow
but it's made of lava, the tidal wave
which sweeps back up the valley in high style
burning all the mosques.
I adapt myself as best I can to this manifestation
of an absurdly miscarried paradise –
much worse than a hell –
from time to time I live in one of my wounds
every moment I change homes
peace always scares me:
       sea-anemone,
       fiery whirlpool of the dust
       of lost worlds,
       having spit the living water of my entrails like a volcano
       I stay with my word-loaves and secret minerals
so I live inside a huge thought
but mostly
prefer to confine myself
in the smallest of my ideas
or perhaps live in a magic formula –
only the first words
the rest being all forgotten –
I live in obstacle
I live in debacle
I live in the lap of a great disaster
most often I live on the dry dug
of the leanest peak – she-wolf of these clouds –

I live in the halo of cactuses
I live in a flock of goats pulling on the teat
of an abandoned almond-tree
to tell the truth I no longer know my exact address
fantastic or terrible
I live in the octopuses' cave
I battle an octopus for an octopus cave
   brother don't insist:
   strands of seaweed
   trapping me in creepers
     or laying me out in Morning Glory
   it's all one
     and that the wave rolls
     the sun cups
     the wind whips
   the round lump of my nothingness

if not atmospheric, historic pressure
makes my wrongs grow beyond measure –
even if it makes some of my words sumptuous

From *Moi, laminaire* 1982

Sony Rupaire (b. 1940, Guadeloupe)
He Started To Laugh

He started to laugh.
And he was like a thatched roof burning
his mouth swallowing the sky his throat wide.
He started to laugh.
The collaborator lash crashed down…
seventeen, eighteen…
He started to laugh.
The bamboo of his body bending like a laden mango-tree
his eyes rolled like begonia flowers,
the clamp of his jaw shut itself on the effort
and the sun broke on the soft rocks of his resentment.
He started to laugh.
The trees in the fields bending over his forehead.
Like a bird of prey the wind turning in the savannah.
Curious, the day leaned down to watch him better.
And the lash crashed down…
twenty-two, twenty-three…
Ah! Ah! Ah! Oh! Oh! Oh! he laughed.
He laughed for his hunger, he laughed for his thirst,
he laughed for his suffering and for his glory,
for those who were laughing, for those who weren't laughing.
He laughed for his fear, for the fear of others,
those who are afraid of being afraid,
afraid of not being able to laugh.
He laughed for himself. He laughed for his own, those the chain
had nailed for ever to the ground, those who were measuring the forest,
                                                                  those
standing guard round the field of canes.
Ah! Ah! Ah! Oh! Oh! Oh! he laughed.
And the lash crashed down…
twenty-five, twenty-six, twenty-seven…
He laughed. He laughed, the negro,
but the measurelessness of his laugh had troubled the peace of the world.

From *Cette igname brisée qu'est ma terre natale ou Gran parade ti cou-baton* 1971

Monchoachi (b. 1946, Martinique)
Embracing You

Embracing you,
earth coming up
through your mouth
you were ceaselessly disgorging earth.
Always embracing you
and your breasts which jeered at the air
under the corsage of pink openwork
taffeta;

for a long time we hoped for this dawn
powdering
what we looked at,
a struck match
lifting itself
glowing
behind the scene.

A long time
since this slow inexhaustible
sadness set in
with tuba backing
while rains fell in torrents
and swallowed themselves into gutters.
Sometimes a fresh cheerful shower
made water splash
from the plum tree onto the corrugated iron.

So you stammered out every word,
together we repeated each word –
how could we be careless
when we knew each was promise
and wound
necessary to both endure
and make good –
then, one after the other,

we hid them under the roses
near gold-dust.

All the measurelessness of nature
in the cursed fig-tree.

From *L'espère-geste* 2002

Right At The Top, Among Pale Water

Right at the top, among pale water,
a stand of straight bamboo,
she wears herself away.

And the rains from the earth
hover and cast a shadow over you.

The heavy pulse of the Earth
which gathers there, comes to terms there,
is wrung out there – a word
lengthening as if at ease, turning blue
in its surroundings, along processions of blue crabs,
along a lapis-lazuli shroud

and a blue moon, prolonging
the Key seduced by the long echo of cicadas
and long frenzy,
the sea-sprays, Aïe! La Cendre,

to infinity.

From *Nuit gagée* 1992

Translated by Clare Durey

CENTREFOLD

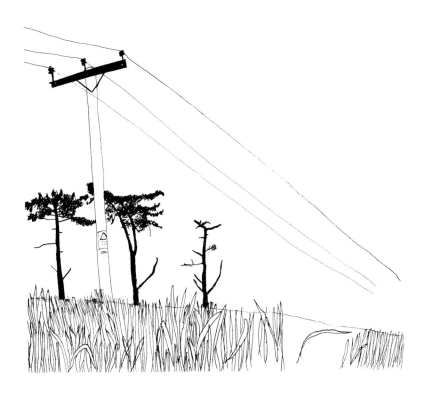

What spaces are considered legitimate for the writer to work in? Why have they been developed and defined, and when and how can the writer usefully transgress them?
    —Michael Schmidt

Close To The Bone:
Elaine Feinstein talks about beginning

In 1997, Michael Schmidt interviewed Elaine Feinstein for *PNReview* (*PNR* 118, available on-line at www.elainefeinstein.com/PNR-interview.pdf). Here, to celebrate Feinstein's latest work, which includes the recent biography of Akhmatova, *Anna of all the Russias* (Weidenfeld and Nicolson, 2005), and her new collection, *Talking to the Dead* (Carcanet, due out in March 2007), we supplement that earlier, in-depth interview with a few questions of our own.

You've talked elsewhere about your own education; but your parents' educational backgrounds were mixed. Judaism is very much a culture of the word. How influential were the attitudes to language and literature with which you grew up?

My mother – a gentle, sensible, woman with a Grammar School education, and brothers who went to Cambridge – taught me to read before I went to school. She was delighted to find me responsive. When she wrote to her brother Jo, then a Director of Education at Ealing, for advice, he told her rather sniffily that if I had any talents they would come out whatever school I went to. Although usually over-awed by Jo, she ignored him on this occasion and sent me to the Wyggeston Grammar School from the age of four. I owe a great deal to that decision.

It is only recently that I have come to understand the extent of her ambition for me. I explained in the interview with Michael Schmidt how I came to be an only child, and how sad that was for her. But it was fortunate for me. Quietly but firmly she wanted me to succeed as a son might have succeeded. At the time (in the thirties and forties) it was not thought a great idea in the Leicester Jewish Community for a daughter to have intellectual interests. She was delighted by every poem in the school magazine, and especially when I won an Exhibition to Cambridge.

If it had not been for the Great War, which eliminated a whole generation of eligible young men, it is unlikely that my mother would have married anyone less than a lawyer or a doctor. Instead, at the age of thirty or so, she was allowed to marry my father in one of his prosperous periods. I have never known exactly what led my wealthy grandfather to strike his daughter out of his Will, but it had something to do with his dislike of my father's extravagance. "If you have a penny, spend a halfpenny," I once heard him say. It was doubtless sensible advice, but not my father's style.

He was ebullient and, if not exactly handsome – he reminded me of Humphrey Bogart – stubbornly flamboyant. I adored his scoffing and gibing, just as I enjoyed his reckless generosity when things went well, and his confidence they would surely improve when they went badly.

My four grandparents were Russian Jews, who arrived in England at the end of the nineteenth century. The two families were very different. My mother's father, a glazier, was a very successful businessman. The grandfather I knew best was a Talmudic scholar, who knew several languages and had no interest whatsoever in business. All my father's family believed God would look after them; while my mother's brothers were militantly atheist, believing only education could put the world to rights. My father left school at twelve and made his own way in the wood trade, first as a cabinet maker and then as manufacturer of wooden goods. I adored him and gave him most of my love, which was very unfair on my mother.

That split between the values of my mother's family and my father's was the source, one way or another, of many of my novels.

I didn't work hard at school until I was about fourteen, when I discovered I could come top in English by bothering a bit. A very good teacher, Miss Adams, urged me to read more widely, and encouraged my early attempts to write poems and stories. There were a group of us who were protected by her and we were good friends; but I lived far more intensely in the world of after-school.

And that I must explain: it was wartime. Leicester, a leafy respectable town before the war, was suddenly filled with London market boys, Hungarian refugees and American servicemen. What brought them into my aegis was that several of them were Jewish, so my father, who was President of the Synagogue, invited them round for meals.

For an only child I was given a surprising amount of liberty. I went to the Palais de Danse most Saturday nights. Sometimes we all played poker. The people I most wanted to like me cared only about clothes, American Jazz and sex, so I wanted to be Lauren Bacall slinking into a dangerous nightclub; to play poker with a cigarette sticking out of my lips; to dance like the Americans could. I concealed the sensitive poetry-loving creature I already was.

Another split. I had poetry and sex in two different baskets, and it took me years to bring them together. I never talked much to my friends about the books I loved. I remember two poets I found on my own outside the school syllabus: T. S. Eliot and Gerard Manley Hopkins. Neither made much sense to my handsome, rakish boyfriends.

The only three years of my life when I didn't write poetry were my undergraduate years in Cambridge, perhaps because F. R. Leavis was such a powerful critical presence then. I had a short story in *Granta*, then edited by Tony Shaffer. But it was a group of men from Trinity, particularly a group of Fulbright Scholars, who taught me about American poetry and modern novels. They were much older than I was, and I was shy at voicing intellectual opinions in their presence. Neither my home nor my social world had prepared me for it.

My closest friend and co-supervisee at Newnham was Audrey Laski, a precociously brilliant girl and a Major Scholar, who took a Triple First in the English Tripos. Her taste in literature for pleasure, surprisingly, ran to Georgette Heyer, Dorothy Sayers and Marjorie Allingham. And women's magazines. (She went on to become a very fine novelist.)

Serious literary friendships only began after my degree, when I edited *Cambridge Opinion*, and founded *Prospect* on an American avant-garde platform. My friends in these ventures included Tony Ward (who wrote *The Tent of God*) and David Leitch – said by Donald Davie to be too clever for his own good – who went on to be a brilliant journalist on the *New Statesman* and *Sunday Times*. As you'll know from the Schmidt interview, I was involved soon afterwards with a group of poets equally infatuated with Black Mountain poetry. They often came and sat on my Trumpington floor. J. H. Prynne paced around. We all contributed to the mimeographed sheets of *The English Intelligencer.*

The range of your activity is unusual for a British poet – or indeed novelist. Do you think this has affected how you're read?

Of course it did. It was much distrusted. Perhaps such a spread of interests, and the use of so many different genres, is more acceptable these days.

It wasn't exactly a choice. My first novel began life as a series of prose pieces for a poetry magazine, and was commissioned as a novel by the brilliant young Hutchinson whizz-kid Michael Dempsey on the strength of a chapter. It was closer to the bone of my own life than the poems I was writing then. Later, this became a key aspiration for my poems.

It was natural for me to turn towards American poetry, because I enjoyed American rhythms and intonations. I started my own magazine to introduce poets such as Charles Olson, Paul Blackburn and Ferlinghetti to an English audience.

Reading is central to your practice.

I read avidly, voraciously. My house is overwhelmed with books. Just recently my asthma took a turn for the worse and I was advised it was absolutely essential to hoover them every week. I'm ashamed to say I read while eating meals, which can be messy. I am mildly reassured by the story that Samuel Johnson once found a fried egg between the leaves of a book.

Where and how has all this fed into your own poetics?

I came across the work of Marina Tsvetaeva while researching a series of lectures I was giving on rhythm at the University of Essex. Pasternak spoke of her in his *Essay in Autobiography* (1957), and described her genius as incomparable. When I read Simon Karlinsky's account of her character, in his early book, I recognised in her many of my own faults: domestic eccentricity, impracticality, and a febrile nature. She existed only in Russian; so I began to make versions of her poems, with the help of Angela Livingstone from the Russian Department of the University of Essex, at first only for myself.

It was a transforming experience. The violence of her emotions and the ferocity of her expression of them released me from English defensive caution. She taught me to see irony as a way of keeping deep feeling at a distance.

Particularly because it famously includes translation, literary biography and criticism, your wider writing activity has positioned you as a literary intellectual; one outside the academy. How do you see such a role working: does is thicken up cultural practice, or popularise, or bridge-build to poetry, for example? Do you see yourself as occupying such a role, or is it in the eye of the beholder?

When I began there was precious little interest in the cross fertilization of cultures. Specialization was the key to academic success. Comparative Literature was not regarded as a serious discipline in Cambridge. The University of Essex was bold in setting up such a Department, with Spanish, Russian and American Literature under the same umbrella. I taught American Literature there for two years.

I was seduced away from the academic world when Hutchinson made me a Devil's offer: three years' salary in return for novels. It seemed miraculous at the time but it was not a hugely sensible decision and a horrendous load of journalism fell on my shoulders as a result of leaving the academic world. Almost all my changes of direction can be attributed to that one decision.

There's no obvious place in a university for me now. I never wrote up my Ph.D on poetics. I'm not a Russianist. My contribution to the study of literature has been characteristically eccentric. I wrote a book about Bessie Smith when I'm neither black nor a singer; and three others about Russian poets when I need help with the Russian language. But in English Literature there is an early book about John Clare; Lawrence and his Women; and the biography of Ted Hughes. All poets, I note. Perhaps I could be a Professor of Poetry? As I reflect on this I am impatient with my own trajectory. These days I would prefer to be part of the mainstream.

What did I know about in depth? ...What I had was a good ear for syllables. And as I always had, I read widely on my own: Whitman, Pound, Reznikoff, Olson but also Dunbar, Wyatt, and Herbert. I was moving in a pre-feminist world, so when I wrote my letter to Charles Olson I signed it E.B. FEINSTEIN, to disguise the fact I was a woman. It did not occur to me then to use my far more English-sounding maiden name of Cooklin. It is possible my whole development would have been different if I had. He replied to me, in a famous letter, as Mr Feinstein.

Now I am not sure if I was innocent or stubborn. I remember the idea of Allen Ginsberg as a poet was mocked in Cambridge. His long, rhythmic paragraphs were dismissed as an ungainly sprawl. But I loved his early lyrics. I wrote an essay about the way he set jarring images against one another in 'Walt Whitman in the Supermarket'. It was in my edition of *Cambridge Opinion* which I called 'The Writer Out of Society'.

Have there been role models?

Not exactly. There have been important lifelong friendships. And generous patrons. Donald Davie – a New Movement poet, as well as a critic and a lecturer at the University of Cambridge – was kind to my unpublished poems. His lectures and his wonderful book *Articulate Energy* were a lodestone, particularly the section where he compares Ezra Pound to Wordsworth. I got to know him through David Leitch and Peter Louizos, two undergraduates who were friends with my husband and I when we lived in Portugal Place.

Portugal Place was an important stage in my life. My husband and I were living in the house of Francis Crick, then in America with his wife Odile. It was a glamorous time for us. My husband had just returned to the academic world after some years in industry; I was supervising undergraduates in the English Tripos. The house was far too big and gradually many friends began to join us there, including several homeless au pairs.

David and Peter admired Thom Gunn (so do I) but I wanted to argue them into seeing the great virtues outside the range of early Movement poetry. To this end, I talked about Wallace Stevens, whom they had not heard of then. They were both supervised by Donald Davie, and when he confirmed my contention that Stevens was a great poet they were absurdly impressed.

Soon afterwards I started up the magazine *Prospect*, which was designed to launch American poets such as Olson, Paul Blackburn, Ferlinghetti and others onto the English scene. David Leitch's friend Tony Ward became my assistant editor and a lifetime friend. There was never enough money, and altogether the publication was an extremely foolish undertaking. That said, the first issue had a number of items which have often been re-published, notably Donald Davie's 'Remembering the Movement' which pointed to the pusillanimous use of irony, frequent words such as "maybe" and "perhaps", and other linguistic means of self-defence.

Donald could not be a role model exactly. He was a Northerner brought up in a Methodist tradition. And writing some of his best poems out of that (see his late book, *To Scorch or Freeze*).

When I met the Americans I admired there were problems, too. Ginsberg felt strongly that any revisions killed inspiration; I enjoy buffing up my work. Ed Dorn, handsome as a white wolf, took my first book of poems to be published by Cape Goliard, but I was too old – and too awkward – to be part of his circle, which included the prettiest girls on the Essex campus.

But at least there were notable American Jewish poets I could learn from: Reznikoff, for instance, who taught me to write about my own family. Louis Zukovsky. Stanley Kunitz. So many others.

You ask about the role Jewishness played in my development as a poet, and I think the liturgy was a very small part of it. What I took in were the spoken phrases of the Yiddish language. At the Wyggeston I was often sent to see a headmistress who prided herself on her ability to reduce a disobedient girl to tears. At home, my father would laugh away her words, saying, "Hob im in bud". This he translated for me as "We have him in a bath". When I was puzzled, he tried to explain. "When you have your enemy in a bath, he is defenceless. So – you don't have to worry about him." Clearly I did not have my headmistress in any such vulnerable situation. But my father's voice, his shrug and the Yiddish phrase were strangely comforting.

Elaine Feinstein
Remembering Old Poets

To be in their presence once was
a shot of adrenalin. Wrinkled or flaccid,
they still exuded pheromones. They seemed
already immortal; we saw their future glory
around their heads like haloes.

Even to stand in the cemeteries where they lay
gave us a frisson of joy. We were so sure
the words of their poems would last,
and that the next generation
would be equally in love with the past.

Wittgenstein

Was it him in the Rex cinema,
that illicit afternoon, watching *Casablanca*
as another B movie? I wanted to believe it.
Nervously taking a short cut past
the bronze of Hermes once in Whewell's Court,

I saw him, though, of course, I did not speak.
Such timid gawking only made you impatient.
Meetings with thinkers were a serious matter. That's why
you hated to leave their presence, why you said unhappily:
Not enough people got to know me.

Unsent E-Mail

When I travel without you, I am no more
than a gaudy kite on a long umbilical.
My flights are tethered by a telephone line
to your Parker Knoll, where you wait
lonely and stoical.

About the Festival: there were no penguins
crossing the road on the North Island,
no whales in Wellington harbour.
The nearest land mass is Antarctica, and
the wind blows straight from there to New Zealand.

Katherine Mansfield lived here as a child
and I've bought gartered stockings in bright colours
to honour her in the character of Gudrun.
For you, I've bought a woollen dressing gown.
You were always home to me. I long for home.

The 2006 StAnza Lecture:
What, How Well, Why?

MICHAEL SCHMIDT

Pitié pour nous qui travaillons aux frontières.
– Apollinaire

Nick Hornby, in *The Polysyllabic Spree* comments, "We are never allowed to forget that some books are badly written; we should remember that sometimes they're badly read, too." It's this issue of reading – partial reading, facile reading, dismissive reading, pious reading, wrong reading – that I want to address. Please don't imagine that I believe there is such a thing as a single reading of a poem, or even a right reading; but we all know that there can be wrong readings, seriously wrong readings, and that the space a poem makes in language is specific in certain ways about which we can agree, even if we don't necessarily agree about what precisely that space contains, or how or why it contains it. We might also agree that reading is an acquired skill, and that when and how we acquire it, and from whom, is relevant to how we do it and to what we do with it.

I'd like also to introduce the words of the American critic Cornel West which my Glasgow colleague Professor Willy Maley drew to my attention. Cornel West is writing in an American context, but *mutatis mutandis* his words have a resonance for me in Britain: "I think for some of us the academy is a subculture of escape – and I'm not using escapism in a pejorative sense – but as an escape from the rampant anti-intellectualism in this country, the fear of critical sensibilities, democratic sensibilities, that is deeply ensconced within the parochialism and provincialism of the very people whom we often invoke."

An early critic took Philip Larkin's 'Church Going' to task: the "*persona*" was inconsistent; he pretended to know *less* than he evidently knew, and the poem ended on an affirmation quite out of key and keeping with where it had set out from. How could a poem move from, "Once I am sure there's nothing going on, I step inside/Letting the door thud shut. Another church" to the astounding stanza beginning, "A serious house on serious earth it is / In whose blent air"? There was not much Larkin about in those days. Only later did it become clear that the essential thing about voices in Larkin's longer – and some of the shorter – poems is that they change: beginning in resistance, a resolutely ironic stance, they develop in relation to experience and reach an understanding or a point from which understanding might be possible. They surprise a hunger in themselves to be more serious.

That early critic was clear-headed, though he was proven wrong. One element in the by-then stiffening legacy of Modernism was the notion of the *persona*, the mask. The poet created a coherent and therefore a consistent mask. That was his task. The rictus grin of the comic mask cannot change. You change expressions by changing masks, by changing roles, by changing voices. And it's always a mistake to associate the voice of the poem with that of the poet. I learned this at school under the aegis of the New Criticism, using that wonderful anthology *Understanding Poetry* which hijacked three generations of American schoolchildren into a specific way of reading. We had the lines, "A poem should not mean / but be" tattooed on our cortex. Had Philip Larkin been less a poet and harkened to his critic (G. S. Fraser, I think it was, writing in *Critical Quarterly*) he would have become, well, other than he did. Fraser compared him, disadvantageously, with Thom Gunn; whose thematic *overload* he contrasted with the philosophical and emotional enervation of Larkin's Church Goer.

Persona, voice: the critical predilection, the convention of one age gradually gives way to that of the next. A change was occurring in the culture of reception even as Larkin, and Fraser, were writing, one inside the poem, the other outside. Larkin was breaking new ground, and Fraser was trying to fit this new ground on to the old map. Fraser's willingness to engage, his sense of something stirring, his courage in risking judgement, is salutary; evidence of a living engagement between the reader and the new text. One of my favourite reviews of all time is Edward Thomas's of Pound's *Personae* in 1909. In it he noted that Pound wrote an English in which it seemed that Shakespeare had never existed, a language swept clear of the semantic encumbrances and associations of the long tradition, fresh and new minted. And he added, with due humility, even apologetically, that he had no critical language for dealing with this new poetry; that a critical language would need to be devised for describing and appraising it. Gordon Bottomley, that honourable, pompous Georgian and little-Englander, was to argue Thomas out of his enthusiasm, but Thomas, as reviewer, had caught the whiff of Modernism and had not stopped his nose against it.

This sort of criticism follows the creative act, responds to and registers it, communicates, to the poet, to the general reader, an informed and considered view. The best critics are those who are willing to follow their judgement rather than merely their taste; who are as it were led by judgement rather than by taste. Two anecdotes. Ernst Gombrich sent his students to the V&A to view the Raphael cartoons. All but one handed in their assignments. The exception said she didn't want to write about the Raphaels because she didn't like them. "I asked you to write about the

Raphael cartoons, not about yourself," he said, and sent her to complete the assignment. He required that self-effacement from his students that I as a teacher ask of mine, and that as an editor and publisher I crave from the general reader. It is the old Coleridgean formula: when you want to understand a work ask first what it's setting out to do, then ask how well it achieves its aim, and finally, only finally, whether it was worth doing. That last question admits the 'I'.

The other anecdote puts Picasso in the frame with an American GI at the end of the Second World War. The soldier said he disliked Picasso's kind of art with its distortions and stylisations and dislocations. "What sort of art do you like?" asked Picasso. The GI pulled out a photograph of his girlfriend and presented it to the artist, who gazed at it and asked, "Is she really this small?" It is about the conventions we are prepared to accept, about conventions so ingrained that we do not recognise them as such; it is about becoming conscious of them, of what is conventional, and understanding why, and what that convention includes and excludes.

Criticism sets out to clear a space for what is new and unexpected, what may be difficult or (as in the case of Thomas's welcome to Robert Frost's work) deceptively simple. Marianne Moore continued to admire in Elizabeth Bishop, even after things cooled between them, the originality she had admired and encouraged critically from the outset: "Some authors do not muse within themselves; they "think" – like the vegetable-shredder which cuts into the life of a thing. Miss Bishop is not one of these frettingly intensive machines. Yet the rational considering quality in her work is its strength – assisted by unwordiness, uncontorted intentionalness, the flicker of impudence, the natural unforced ending. Hers is an art which" (she quotes a poem of Bishop's) "'cuts its facets from within.'" Often criticism has to praise what is not: all those "un-s" have a Hardyesque, or a Housmanesque feel.

In all these instances, there was a culture of reception in which original achievement and change could be registered. There was a complex and diverse review culture, something which is only just being redeveloped now thanks to the web and to excellent on-line journals such as *Jacket*, coming to supplement the old stalwarts and replace the journals that have folded. A culture of reception, it seems to me, is public, not contained within the academy, though academics and theorists are welcome to contribute to it. Terry Eagleton in *Stand* was one of the best, most consistent, severe and generous, of the critics of new poetry I encountered when I first came to Britain. Another was the *Guardian*'s Martin Dodsworth. It is through the culture of reception that interested general readers find out about new books or rediscover old, that writers see themselves reflected, recognisably, unrecognisably... We are talking 'reader development' in an early sense: appraisal and judgement intended not to sell the idea of reading, and therefore always recommending, but to make sure that new works and editions are valued, that the factitious, meretricious and merely conventional are identified as such. Culture has value only if it is informed and sets out to inform; if it takes positive and negative risks, and if it is willing to risk giving offence in the interests of truth, for example, to insist on the quality of, say, Geoffrey Hill's sometimes resistant work, in the face of three decades' neglect and mis-evaluation. Poetry's mere cheerleaders do the art more harm than good. They are in a way the real censors because they discourage engagement, shrouding the poem in good will.

That culture of neglect and misevaluation was a curious one. I put it in the past tense because I want to believe it is passing. It was a culture in which weakness was made to look like strength; narrow-mindedness and worse, narrowing-mindedness, praised themselves as common sense and were made to seem decisive, to cut the crap, to speak "with respect". They forgot, as we are beginning to remember, that the sense that makes poetry is anything but common.

The culture of reception is of course never single, thank goodness. The critical diversity that greeted Modernism was healthy, from the extreme rejections to the extreme advocacies, from Arthur Waugh to Ezra Pound. Reaction against Modernism continued and continues, with increasing stridency here and abroad, suggesting that it was a dreadful mistake, a long detour (by way of America) and a distraction from a fundamentally British way. The compass was set in that direction decisively by some fine poets, among them A. E. Housman.

Housman expressed his *public* attitude to poetry most fully in a lecture, 'The Name and Nature of Poetry', delivered in Cambridge in 1933. Housman was male, and white, an academic and a great classical scholar. But he was also hostile, intensely so, to the new poetry and to those things in which it declared itself to be rooted, and so he spoke for much of Britain then, and now. That is why he, and Philip Larkin, also a white, male, university employee, are so often called as witnesses in the case *against* Modernism and its kinds of critical engagement.

Such criticism paints clothes on the naked emperor, they argue; it understands and therefore forgives all that is new and experimental; most of all, such criticism, because it is, or pretends to be, subtle, discredits, devalues, misvalues, or worst, ignores work that is conventional, mainstream, that appeals to the market.

What we must trust, Housman insists, are our instincts, which are, in his view at least, genuine, unconditioned, fresh; which are value-free in a singularly Rousseauvian sense. Just as we must not turn the dark probe of criticism on that bright, vulnerable object, the poem, so we must not turn it on the reader either, because that might darken the spontaneity and physicality of his response, it might suggest that taste be tempered or re-directed by judgement, for if it isn't it tends to atrophy, and a comfortable, terrible conservatism can be born.

Housman condemned the "difficult" poetry of the Metaphysicals, back in vogue at the time; and by implication discredited the new poetry of the twentieth century. Poetry was for him less an intellectual than a physical experience, and it seems that the intellectual faculties had little part to play in taking or registering the effect of a poem. He was a prime specimen of the literary Manichee, a marvellous and deliberate technician within specific elegiac and lyrical modes, with a limited thematic range and a plangency which touches anyone's heart. His work is back-lighted: that is to say, all of its tropes, its generic and technical resources, have classical authority. Like Thomas Gray he was a master-pasticheur who also happened to be a master. His roots were in Greek literature, like Pound's and H.D.'s, but he was a wholly different sort of plant.

The poetry that he approved took hold of him, engaged him, at a level he could not, or rather would not, intellectually plumb. A poem's effect had to do with music, rhyme and emotional direction, not with teasing out *meaning*.

> Poetry indeed seems to me more physical than intellectual. A year or two ago, in common with others, I received from America a request that I would define poetry. I replied that I could no more define poetry than a terrier can define a rat, but that I thought we both recognised the object by the symptoms which it provoked in us. One of those symptoms was described in connexion with another object by Eliphaz the Temanite: "A spirit passed before my face: the hair of my flesh stood up." Experience has taught me, when I am shaving of a morning, to keep watch over my thoughts, because, if a line of poetry strays into my memory, my skin bristles so that the razor ceases to act. This particular symptom is accompanied by a shiver down the spine; there is another which consists in a constriction of the throat and a precipitation of water to the eyes; and there is a third which I can only describe by borrowing a phrase from one of Keats's last letters, where he says, speaking of Fanny Brawne, "everything that reminds me of her goes through me like a

spear". The seat of this sensation is the pit of the stomach.

Most of us would probably concur that what Philip Larkin calls the "lift-off" point in a poem, if it has one, can provoke one of these three localised effects, though we might wish to add several: a shaking of the sides with comic poetry, a sexual stirring in other contexts. There are many more. The poet Laura Riding helped Michael Roberts compose the introduction to the definitive anthology of its time, the *Faber Book of Modern Verse*. They insisted there that "the poetic use of language can cause discord as easily as it can cure it. A bad poem, a psychologically disordered poem, if it is technically effective may arouse uneasiness or nausea or anger in the reader." Here are some more effects to add to Housman's list, bad ones as well as good. A poem can have *actual* consequences for readers. A poem can make something happen.

Housman's theories – or prejudice – answered a deep prejudice in his audience. They signify primarily as they relate to his own verse and the classical work he liked best, but his admirers gave them wider credence. Here was an unanswerable, because instinctive and unanalysable, case against those rebarbative experiments that threatened the coherence and continuity of English poetry. The young critic I. A. Richards (who was unfortunately also white, male and an academic) left the lecture muttering, "Housman has put the clock back thirty years!"

At the time that I was establishing *PNReview*, I was still close to the Mexican literary scene in which I grew up. It was a period of intellectual questioning and liberalisation in Latin America. The tight fist of a cultural Marxism or Stalinism that insisted on a narrow national focus, strict solidarity between writers, and on affirmative and realist art, was loosening its hold. Latin American Modernists were beginning to be read again, and Octavio Paz was beginning to be dug out from under the opprobrium with which Pablo Neruda and others had darkened him. Literary culture was deeply politicised, as how could it not be with so large and sinister a neighbour to the North, and it had resisted interrogating Stalinism for fear (understandable if not honourable) of appearing complicit with reactionary or American interests. It was specifically Paz's early essay on the Gulag, published in Victoria Ocampo's magazine *Sur* in Buenos Aires, that had so offended Neruda. Poet and essayist, Octavio Paz was a long-serving diplomat who knew writers from across the globe and was steeped in the literature of the present and past, east and west. He had given up his diplomatic post at the time of the Olympic Massacre in Mexico in 1968. He edited the magazine *Plural* and, when that was closed by a combination of state and commercial censorship, he opened a new magazine called *Vuelta* or

Return. Paz insisted, from his classic anthropological study *The Labyrinth of Solitude* onwards, that Mexicans needed to know who they were, where their culture had come from, how they were perceived from abroad, how theirs fit in among the wider cultures of Latin America and the world. He wanted Mexican writers to be part of the larger discourse of the day. "Criticism," he insisted, "is the beginning of freedom of imagination." This was no pious credo in a country where such freedom had been limited for years, though the great tradition of public mural painting had become established and certain practitioners of the plastic arts had prospered (though others had starved or emigrated).

Paz meant that a reader, as much as a writer, needs to be aware of what the limiting 'decorums', if we may call them that, of the age are. The eighteenth century had stylistic decorums, rules about which registers of language, what fields of reference, were appropriate for different genre. We have decorums of a different kind; if we identify them we become aware of what we are accepting without reflection, what we are choosing, what we are complicit with, and what that complicity entails, and excludes. Some of the modern decorums are political, some aesthetic, some sexual, some ethnic. What spaces are considered legitimate for the writer to work in? Why have they been developed and defined, and where and how can the writer usefully transgress them? To take an example less remote than Mexico, when Eavan Boland began writing in Ireland, she declares, it was possible to have a political murder in a poem but not a baby. Whole areas of experience – gendered and not – and areas of memory were excluded, and her creative endeavour necessarily entailed an enabling critical endeavour.

Her experience is analogous to Eliot's and Pound's in making space in Britain and Ireland for renewal in writing; and to Adrienne Rich's. In short, a writer might be expected to be aware of the decorums, imposed from without, or inertly there; or imposed from within, as in the case of Allen Ginsberg, self-censoring his work before *Howl* out of a reticence about coming out to his father. What the authorities – parents, editors, critics, the police, the funding bodies who are subsidising the writers themselves or the means of production, what the censors, the church, and readers themselves – might expect, are things best *understood* so that they can be allowed for or resisted.

I am talking of the *agora* here; the market place in the wider sense that it had before it was so thoroughly deculturised in the 1970s and 1980s, when economics decisively displaced politics and politics displaced aesthetics. Or so it can seem. That displacement is closer than it should be, and I mean closer in more than just a chronological sense. Its values have affected, even corrupted, the language of teaching and the expectations of institutions and individuals. The last time I saw Malcolm Bradbury at a conference at UEA, he was reflecting ruefully on the way in which a programme created to give writers and would-be writers a space in which to experiment, learn about and further their craft had become decisively 'outcome-orientated', the chief outcome being to feed work into a publishing industry with very specific requirements and markets. The outcome orientation naturally affected recruitment decisions, as in any business.

What does this have to do with poetry? Everything, I would say. In the short and the long term, if we want a grown-up readership for poetry, able and willing to tell a hawk from a handsaw, and if we want our poets to develop and grow without pollarding, trellising, pruning, grafting, we need a diverse and vigorous culture of reception.

W. H. Auden understood what the pressures on a writer can be when that culture of reception becomes unitary and coercive, and how it is necessary, if one is to grow, to make tracks. In 1939 he emigrated to the United States, leaving his admirers and their over-insistent politics behind. What marks the Auden who obtained his freedom is a refusal to conform, to come down from his brilliant linguistic and cultural perch, to trim. What is a highbrow? he asks in an early piece. "Someone who is not passive to his experience but who tries to organise, explain and alter it, someone in fact, who tries to influence his history: a man struggling for life in the water is for the time being a highbrow. The decisive factor is a conflict between the person and his environment…" That conflict occurs in art; it also occurs in criticism.

"Poetry is not concerned," Auden says, "with telling people what to do, but with extending our knowledge of good and evil, perhaps making the necessity for action more urgent and its nature more clear, but only leading us to the point where it is possible for us to make a rational and moral choice." Poetry is still instrumental; and that word *rational* is there, virtually synonymous with *moral*.

The criticism I quoted at the beginning of this lecture is specific and local, but is also evidence of adjustment, of growth, of education in its etymological sense of leading on, leading away, leading forward. Underpinning such criticism are attitudes of mind, value systems; strata in which inertia is the rule. And in penetrating, understanding and undermining those strata, criticism plays a crucial part. If they remain undisturbed, a great conformity can be seen to settle on a culture, of a kind which some believe may already be with us today in ways we ought to register, to resist if we can, or to wave a white flag and surrender.

I'd like to consider some of the decorums, the received ideas, under which we labour as readers and poets, as teachers and editors. I will advance obliquely because the subjects are treacherous and I am a vulnerable critical specimen – being male, academic etc.

1. Pluralism and Multiculturalism

When Michael Hamburger described Pound and Eliot as "Americans at odds with the pluralism of their own native culture," he got it quite wrong. It was the drab assimilativeness of that culture that they were at odds with, an assimilativeness which over the last two decades we have endeavoured to reproduce in Britain. The multiculturalisms of Modernism or modernisms, from the anthropological adventures of Lawrence and Joyce to the deliberately non-assimilative strategies of Pound and Eliot, of Hugh MacDiarmid and David Jones – their fascination with the values and truths of cultures other than their own and their refusal to appropriate or "translate" that otherness – are a manifest of cultural pluralism generally despised because it insists on the unfamiliar and seems thus to be "elitist": those chunks of Greek, Chinese, Sanskrit, Welsh and Lallans, the differentiated speech of Madame Sosostris, Thomas Jefferson, the Black GI, Old Possum, Brutus and the shipwright. Within British literature, I for one prefer the sense of Persia and Japan that I get from Bunting, or of Russia that I get in the powerful translations of MacDiarmid and Morgan into Scots, to the more accommodating and accommodated assimilations of Hughes, for example. Applying familiar templates to the unfamiliar is a Colonial and Imperial strategy; it was the Modernists who refused to play that game, celebrating the irreducible otherness of the other. To speak of Eliot's "allusions" to the Sanskrit, for example, is to give *The Waste Land* short shrift. The Sanskrit elements are not there in a decorative spirit; they are there because of the complementarity of that other culture, which Eliot sought to understand because it might provide a stability against the tottering instabilities of post-War Europe.

2. Politics

In the market place poetry is required to evince a conscience, and often conscience of a specific kind, in relation to 9/11, to the wars in Afghanistan and Iraq, to nuclear power and other issues.

In objecting to Anglophone Modernists, we generally, and understandably, object to what we see as their politics; and it is the case that in Lewis and Pound, as in a different way in Eliot and Joyce and Yeats, in Lawrence and beyond, there was a tendency to project aesthetic categories on to the political screen, to envision an order in society congruent with the selection and stylisation of art. The romantic model, organic and individual, had been displaced by lucent geometries, and the values of humanism and individualism (apart from the individualism of the artist, whom they privileged) were not top of the Modernist list of priorities much of the time:

> Compleynt, compleynt, I hearde upon a day
> Artemis singing, Artemis, Artemis
> Agaynst Pity lifted her wail:
> Pity causeth the forests to fail,
> Pity slayeth my nymphs,
> Pity spareth so many an evil thing.
> Pity befouleth April,
> Pity is the root and the spring.
> Now if no fayre creature followeth me
> It is on account of Pity . . .

(Pound, opening of *Canto* XXX)

The great contemporary Irish poet Thomas Kinsella's critical approach to such issues in Yeats is exceptional and enabling: yes, he concedes, there are problematic elements in 'A Bronze Head' and other pieces in Last Poems. "...Yeats's 'true' political position is readily ascertainable, but it is only one of the poem's working parts."

Certainly the aestheticisation of politics was a dreadful triumph of imagination, a triumph of Shelleyan proportions. In a later age, the defeat of imagination can look dreadful, too: when it loses its bearings and its energy, and analytical strategies that follow from politics annex the aesthetic realm. This equally disenables writers and readers; it closes down categories of reading, zones of formal experiment and endeavour.

3. Voice

Laura Riding strongly criticised what must be the dominant decorum of the mainstream today, and certainly of the writing schools: the compulsion that each writer must find a voice, an inflection, a dialect, a way of speaking specific to the person, so that the writing has a voice-print that is sincere and recognisable. This cultivation of eccentricity, or this refusal to agree that there is a centre in which discourses meet, a communion, is a deep-rooted prejudice marked by a politics of individualism. Laura Riding suggested that the voice that matters is that of Wordsworth's "a man (or woman) talking to men (and women)" rather than "this particular man (or woman)" talking to men (and women). The deliberate self-individuation of her contemporaries repelled her: their writing put personality before language in a spirit of self-display. The poem became, even on the page, merely performance; the freedoms Larkin earned for the voice in time, for the changing and changeable voice, were first exaggerated and then systematised.

Poems generally come more out of an engagement with language, and with poetry, than with life; life provides occasions, but what matters in the end is less the grain of sand than the pearl itself. Frederic Raphael, trailing a very long coat, says "Sincerity is the thumb-print of the amateur." This is not to say that *integrity* is *de trop*: integrity and sincerity in art are quite distinct and even at times inimical categories.

4. The past in its relation to the present

Eliot's essay 'Tradition and the Individual Talent' remains a point of reference, but what it proposes is preached and taught against both inside and outside the academy. The Bergsonian, and the Proustian, notion of our inseparability from the past, the theory, or perception, of *durée,* might be reaffirmed. What we are includes, and depends upon, what we have been; what we have been can be changed not in pattern but in meaning by what we become. Life by the chronological clock versus life by values. Not to know what we are made of is not to know who we are; is possibly *to fall victim to* what we are made of. The poet who refuses to read other poetry for fear of being influenced has been influenced and will write without knowing how derivative the work is, for the ear is not innocent and memory is a faulty filter.

5. Subjection

Today the wannabe poet progresses like the academic, the civil servant, the manager, up a series of marked steps to become a member of the fraternity and sorority of Published Poets. The *obedience* such an ascent requires can be at odds with the very principles of the art. It is an art of speculation not in the old sense but entirely in the new, speculating on the prize, the publisher, the public – poetry has become as keen to embrace the main chance as the basest prose.

MacDiarmid, MacLean, MacCaig, Morgan, Crichton Smith, Lochhead and others represented to me a core but diverse Scottish tradition, certain of its place and therefore confident to entertain the other, building out and where it could over, towards Europe and the Americas and Asia, back and forward in time; recognising the elements in and of their tradition as enabling them to effect these endeavours of transcendence. "In my own back yard," they seemed to say, realising how commodious that back yard is, how different from the tidied back yard of the neighbour to the south, with which they share elements of language. One of the reasons I wanted to come to Scotland to teach was that I had the impression of a culture quite distinct from the English culture in which, or against which I had worked, for thirty-odd years. I imagined that here hostility to Modernism and post-Modernism, categories enormously diverse and rich and embracing a number of Scotland's greatest practitioners, would be less insistent than in England where it seemed to me to be a manifestation of a fear of culture. But that old defensive insularity has infected much of the larger nation, as if the process of eighteenth-century self-colonisation so brilliantly evoked by Robert Crawford in his 1992 study *Devolving English Literature*, had revived. Larkin's tones, ironies, dismissive asides, displace not only MacDiarmid but MacLean, MacCaig, Graham and Morgan. The dying fall is applauded. Modernism and post-Modernism are dismissed in aphorisms. The literal and the banal are privileged. As for the sublime, talk to the hand. Such gestures of rejection magnify figures no larger than those in the photographs which the American GI shared with Picasso.

Surely we can, without necessarily being academic, but using imagination, distance ourselves from excesses committed almost a century ago; and also perhaps put a little distance between ourselves as writers, demand a little less solidarity, a little less local backslapping, more debate and engagement, at the same time giving the reader less of a condescending embrace? Down with the poetry cheerleaders, I say! Readers don't need to be talked down to, some do not need to be sold on poetry. It's possible to become impatient with the mundane sense of freedom that some writers are content to seek, the tackiness and short take of much of our reading culture, the condescension of our performance culture.

Poems, *pace* Housman, do not exhaust themselves in gooseflesh, a tear, or a tightening of the stomach. Housman's poems themselves are not so readily spent. Robert Graves spoke out against what he called an "Age of Acquiescence". Acquiescence is to be resisted, in particular acquiescence in the programme of market development pursued by those who believe poetry is a good, however good or bad the poems are.

We live in a nation of countless poets and a limited number of poetry readers; we have a great critical tradition from which we are licensed to avert our gaze as from something stuffy, musty, disabling. Yet almost all the critics I have quoted from in this lecture are poets, and not one of them has been less than deeply engaged in the art and the issues, artistic, political and other, that surround it. All of them are, as critics and publishers and editors and teachers, members of the dreaded police you heard about last year, and their patrol is edifying, sustaining, challenging. To chide them for their colour, gender, education, is as much as to silence them for being who they are. One is put in mind of Ring Lardner's quip: "*Shut up*, he explained."

On March 17 2006 Michael Schmidt gave the fifth annual StAnza Lecture at the StAnza Festival, St Andrews. This is an abridged version. Previous speakers have included Neil Astley, in 2005.

The Journey Or The Dance?
On Syllables Belonging To Each Other

RUTH PADEL

Ezra Pound called the process of making a poem the "dance of the intellect among the words". Charles Olson refined that. "The dance of the intellect", he said, "is among the syllables." The syllable, "the minim and source of speech", is the "king and pin" of poetry. Worry, he told poets, about "the syllable, that fine creature". It is the syllable, not rhyme and metre, that "leads the harmony on".

"The syllable, that fine creature"

So what is a syllable? The word comes from the Greek verb *sullambano*. *Sun* means "with". *Lambano* is a large violent verb, meaning "grab hold" physically or mentally. Compounds of it often mean things like "comprehend": an English word that comes from a Latin equivalent to *sullabano*: *cum* means *with*, *prehendo* means "seize, lay hold of". *Sullambano* means "collect", with the same spread of meanings that word has in, say Jane Austen. "I collect", meaning "I gather, I understand". Physically, *sullambano* means "take with" you, "put together, combine"; "arrest, lay hands on". In speaking and listening, it means "say several things in one word", or "grasp the meaning" of something. So you have several root meanings wriggling at the bottom of this verb. A physical taking and holding, the combining of different elements, and understanding,

All this bears on the noun, *syllabe*. Which has an active sense ("mental grasp" – a realization, a putting two and two together) and a passive one: "that which is held together". This is the sense the Greek grammarians wanted. *Sullabe*: "several letters taken together in one sound". Our "syllable".

But for syllables in poems, we should remember the active sense too. A syllable on its own (if you could have such a thing) is something *held together* by letters. But a syllable in a poem makes relationships with all the other syllables. It is these relationships which hold the poem together. "Syllables rule and hold the line", said Olson. "Listening for the syllables is everything".

One particular syllable rules R.S. Thomas's poem 'Blackbird'.

Blackbird

Its eye a dark pool
in which Sirius glitters

and never goes out.
Its melody husky
as though with suppressed tears.
Its bill is the gold
one quarries for amid
evening shadows. Do not despair
at the stars' distance. Listening
to blackbird music is
to bridge in a moment chasms
of space-time, is to know
that beyond the silence
which terrified Pascal
there is a presence whose language
is not our language, but who has chosen
with peculiar clarity the feathered
creatures to convey the austerity
of his thought in song.

This is a short poem on a huge subject, the existence of God. The first part has ritualizing repetitions like an ancient Welsh riddle poem: *Its, Its, Its*. (The answer to the riddles is the title word.) Halfway through the eighth line comes the pastoral command (reminding us Thomas was a priest), *do not despair*. At first sight, the word *is* in the second part seems to balance the repeated *its* of the first. *Listening[...] is to bridge*; *listening* also *is to know*. But syntactically the third *is* is different. It depends on a verb, *know*. It refers to what we know: *that there is a presence*. The fourth *is* again depends on what has just gone. Language and syntax are becoming more complex: a relative clause, then a further relative dependent on that. This fourth *is* refers to the *language* of the *presence*: it *is not our language*.

Throughout this second part, *is* shifts its place in the line. End-word in the tenth line, penultimate beat in the twelfth, second word in the fifteenth, first word in the sixteenth. But the first part opened without *is*. *Is* only appeared in the third "riddle". We began with the absence of the key existence word. In the second part, *is* dodges about: it is a shifting presence.

The poem is about whether God *is*, or not. Pascal's wager was religious insurance policy. If you believe in God and He exists, fine. If you don't believe and He doesn't, also fine. But what if you don't believe and He does exist? That is what *terrified Pascal*. The bet was on His existence. But this poem is not cynical. It moves from the blackbird's *eye* and *melody* to refusing *despair*; from *listening* to *knowing*. It is a journey into faith that God *is*. So *is* is the crucial syllable. The poem plays with it, withholding it, letting it creep in, balancing it against the repetitions of *its*, letting it extend and depend on the growth of more complex thought. Through it, the poem restates the unspoken question, Does God exist? in terms of syllables and their relationships. Is there a stable place for *is* in the line is a way of saying, Is there a place for God's existence in our lives?

The last line gestures back to the riddles of the first part by answering this in a word that rhymes with *is*. The musical answer, appropriate for a poem whose last word is *song*, is the relation of *is* and *his*.

Relationships of syllables

Poetry in English today is wonderfully various, but all good poems, mainstream, modernist, mad or sane, work by harmonizing syllables, playing with them, laying them cheek to cheek. That is how poems get words to feel right together and so produce – well, Olson used the word beauty. Syllables, he said, let words "juxtapose in beauty". We might just as well say, "in meaning" or "in music". It is the relationships of syllables that makes music, beauty and meaning. The music is the meaning. The meaning is the music.

This has been true of good poems since Homer. "Harmony" comes from the Greek verb *harmottein*, "fit together". It may have referred originally to how you "made" the strings' pegs "fit" in the lyre. But *harmonia* soon came to mean how you tuned your lyre, what "mode" you tuned it to. Then it became an image of all things working together. Chorus members in a dance and song. Citizens in the city, humours in the body. (Orpheus draws everything and everyone to him, brings them together.), It was a key Greek image, medically, socially, morally. In a line of Greek poetry, the "fitting together" of syllables makes the metrics, the meaning and beauty.

The big difference from us is that in rhythms of Greek poetry before the Byzantine period, stress did not matter, whereas in English poems stress is what we listen *for*. A musician recently told me tango is the only dance where the dancers follow the melody not the beat. If that is true, it flies against the habit of the modern Western ear which says *Find order, meaning and pattern, by the beat.*

The accents on Greek words had nothing to do with the rhythm of a line, which was based on the number of feet and syllable-count: the patterning of long and short. In an English line, the beat is the ordering principle. A poet can gather syllables up like flowers, squash them all into the vase of the foot and it doesn't matter. As long as you have five beats in a pentameter, never mind the count. But Greek poetry was stricter. You *could* substitute some syllable patterns for others, but only in some places in the line. And only in metres where the line is always the same (epic's dactylic hexameter, the iambic hexameter of tragic dialogue). Lyrics, where lines kept changing, were much more exacting.

This was such a delicate structure that the art of understanding it waned with the art of composing it. Later Greek philologists invented line divisions ("colometry") to explain it; but they come long after the poets and are not authoritative. Some lyrics, particularly for solo voice, were astrophic: complex, wayward, stanza-less, like jazz cadenzas. Choral lyric was mainly strophic. Stanzas came in pairs and every syllable of the second, the antistrophe, mirrored those of the first, the strophe, exactly. This is "responsion": the syllables correspond, antistrophe "answers" strophe, which means "turn". The antistrophe was a "turn back". The patternings of syllable, intricate as the Alhambra, were expressed in melody and dance: the chorus made responsion clear by singing the strophe to (say) the right, performing gestures meanwhile, then turning to sing the antistrophe at the left, mirroring the gestures exactly. The poet ordered it all. Wrote the music, trained the chorus. Euripides was composer and choreographer (and singer), with a deeply physical musical relationship to the words of which he was the architect.

In our poetry, it is still syllables that make words feel right together, but we use the speech-stress of syllables in a word to feel the order of a line. The ear listens for a beat among the syllables. Syllables say hello over the stanzas and lines, and so relate significantly the words they inhabit.

They may do this by repeating rhythmic patterns (say, a combination of dactyls), but it is above all vowel sounds that hold a poem together and establish its harmony. You can't sing a consonant: you sing vowel sounds. (Consonants divide them.) Vowel sounds generate most types of rhyme (except for consonant rhyme), and rhyme is one of the central things by which words get to belong together. Rhyme satisfies the ear. (Our ear: ancient Greeks would have none of it). That is the point of rhyme. It ties a bow on things, musically and emotionally, by making a relationship between two words which then feels right and significant.

We all get fed up with people asking "do you use rhyme"? Poets "use" rhyme all the time: half-rhyme, consonant rhyme, vowel-rhyme; internal rhymes, random rhymes, words which echo each other from inside one line and across to another, even across stanzas. Oh and there's end-rhyme too. Rhyme is a fundamental way of making words greet each other. It is one way, but not the only way, of getting syllables to make relationships between words.

This poem by Julia Darling, about living with someone you love, was written as she was dying of cancer, so the living and the love have an incalculably powerful charge. It is a sonnet whose shape is ruled by apartness as well as union – to suit the title image of 'Two Lighthouses' either side of a river, connected by *light*, by *signs*. The lines fly apart. There is no rhyme scheme. The two lines of each couplet stay together because they want to, because they have things in common.

Two Lighthouses

I would like us to live like two lighthouses
at the mouth of a river, each with her own lamp.

We could see each other across the water,
which would be dangerous, and uncrossable.

I could watch your shape, your warm shadow,
moving in the upper rooms. We would have jokes.

Jokes that were only ours, signs and secrets,
flares on birthdays, a rocket at Christmas.

Clouds would be cities, we would look for omens,
and learn the impossible language of birds.

We would meet, of course, in cinemas, cafés,
but then, we would return to our towers,

knowing the other was the light on the water,
a beam of alignment. It would never be broken.

(from *Apology for Absence*, Arc Publications, 2005)

In each couplet here, specific syllables interact with specific images to distinguish that couplet from the others, and suggest what each line has in common with its partner while contributing to the whole poem's onward flow. The first has the IV of *live* and *river*, the images of *lighthouses* and *lamp*. The second has the water, and an echo between *water* and *uncrossable* which is picked up in the OR between *watch* and *warm* in the third; but this third is also distinguished by its image of the *shape* in the *rooms*, the hint of physicality. After this suggestion of bodies, the fourth, central couplet (knitted to the third by the repeated *jokes*) has the intimacy of things *that were only ours* and is distinguished musically by the chime of *ours* and *flares*, the K of *jokes, secrets, rocket* and *Christmas*, the long O of *jokes* and *only*, the chime of *secrets* and *Christmas*.

The last six lines, the sestet, turn to the outside and look up. The fifth couplet, with chiming final syllables (*cities, language*), looks to the sky (*clouds, birds*), bringing in the outside world. The sixth lets the pair meet in that world. Instead of the previous lines' easy flow, the comma, after the first syllable and in the first line after the second beat, distinguishes this stanza rhythmically. It brings in hesitation, as if these two operate most easily when separate – but, as we see in the last couplet, secure in *knowing* what the other is to them. This last couplet picks up earlier images: *light, water*. Rhythmically, *never* picks up *other*. Musically, the long I ties *light* and *alignment* together. Conceptually, the *light* is the *alignment*. These people are each other's *alignment*, imaged by the alignment of partner lines in separate couplets through the poem. A complete braiding of image, idea and feeling, sound and line, in which the relationship of syllables plays a key role.

Poems are movement

Poems are made of movement (Charles Olson called relations between syllables "kinetic"). The units of a line are "feet": poems are movement of sound as well as thought. Homer's "paths of song" metaphor reflects the forward impetus of any effective poem. Actors learning a Shakespeare speech think in terms of its journey, where it is going. You move through structure: "stanzas" are "rooms"; a poem is a house and you move, the thought moves, through the rooms in turn.

When frightened (dentist, injections, operations) I have always said poems to myself, and travelling through jungle looking for tigers I realized why. In Laos I had to go three hundred miles through trackless jungle by kayak. I was terrified of rapids, and learned this Emily Dickinson poem to steady me:

> Civilization – spurns – the Leopard!
> Was the Leopard – bold?
> Deserts – never rebuked her Satin –
> Ethiop – her Gold –
> Tawny – her Customs –
> She was Conscious –
> Spotted – her Dun Gown –
> This was the Leopard's Nature – Signor –
> Need – a keeper – frown?
> Pity – the Pard – that left her Asia –
> Memories – of Palm –
> Cannot be stifled – with Narcotic –
> Nor suppressed – with Balm.

I learned as we went. Right paddle down – *Civilization* – next rock – *spurns the leopard* – left paddle, bump down chute – *was the leopard* – spin, crunch on shallow basin, jerk forward, hoosh sideways down waterfall – *bold?* As we went, I asked it what it was about. One, isolation. *Civilization spurns* her. Two, her own nature, *tawny*, wild, *spotted*: not like others. When she's alone, that doesn't matter, *deserts* don't *rebuke* her. Should a man – a *Signor, keeper*, some male guardian of convention – complain about her nature? No – this maculate *dun gown* is what she really is, she won't pretend to be otherwise. Three, loss. This *pard* has *lost her Asia*, some experience she treasures. Four, her *memories* of it will not to be *stifled* or *suppressed*, even if they hurt. As I and my guide emptied the kayak on a slimy bank I thought, it is about being who she is. Isolated, and never mind what people think. No blocking memories just because they hurt. It is a lesson in bravery.

Later, coming down a Sumatran mountain in equatorial jungle nearing sunset, we lost the path and had to slide hundreds of metres through bushes. Even hand-holds you knew to be rotten could steady you for the second it took to find a foothold. Momentum was all. If you stopped, despair hit. My guide was out of sight ahead. I was alone with vegetation and God knows what else but it included three species of cobra, two of them spitting types. Again that poem kept me going. Saying it over and over, I felt I knew why Dickinson put those dashes. Each phrase was just enough for a breath, before the next search for snake-free handhold. The dashes were momentum, rhythm: a pause to collect yourself, make sure of the next movement. I would never have got through without that poem, I clung to it mentally, moved to its rhythm physically. The dashes found me hand-holds and foot-holds.

Sullambano again. Everything about how a poem moves and coheres is about holding and understanding, Holding together, keeping going. As with Euripides, so with Dickinson: a poem's meaning is musical and bodily. Syllables are physical molecules of movement. By the end I felt I knew physically not only what that poem was about – survival – but that this is what poems are: forward movement through dangerous tangle.

Movement of syllables: the dance of many journeys

That was forward movement. Every good poem is a forward journey. There are many types of journey. Pilgrimage. Quest. The inner journey, in all its spiritual, emotional, and psychological weight (sinking in to the unconscious, memory, the past, going into the dark to learn). But there are other sorts of movement than straight on. "On a huge hill", says Donne in *Satires* 3,

Cragged and steep, Truth stands, and he that will
Reach her, about must, and about must go.

About and about? Some poems are about return, like the *Odyssey*. 'Little Gidding' blends the image of pilgrimage into that of return. Return is a new way of seeing where we began:

We shall not cease from exploration
And the end of all our exploring
Will be to arrive where we started
And know the place for the first time.

A poem may not only wind but circle in "ring composition". The movement of syllables in a poem is also, as Euripides training his chorus must often have thought, a dance. (See Pound's "dance of the intellect".) The Little Gidding master, describing how a poem moves, says words support each other in the dance of a poem:

The end is where we start from. And every phrase
And sentence that is right (where every word is at home,
Taking its place to support the others [...]
The complete consort dancing together)
Every phrase and every sentence is an end and a beginning [...]

There are many different sorts and directions of dance as well as journey. Waltz, hip-hop, tango, dervish dance: a poem can do them all. One way of reconciling the journey, the forward movement, of a poem with its dance is by seeing it as a dance of many different sorts of trajectory. Journeys of image, vowel sound, consonant sound, particular rhythms; verbs, interrogatives, pronouns, adjectives: lots of different journeys intersecting like migrating birds or clubbers on the dance floor.

The following poem by J. H. Prynne comes from a collection (*Poems*, Fremantle Arts Centre Press and Bloodaxe Books, 2005) full of love, geology, and reflections on human connection. Its vision of the fluidity of human ties is reflected in the fluid relationships between words, syllables and meanings. The central movement is a walk over *rough grass* of a city to *a concrete path*. Its heart is the *loved side of a temple.*

The Holy City

Come up to it, as you stand there
that the wind is quite warm on the sides
of the face. That it is so, felt
      as a matter of practice, or
      not to agree. And the span,
to walk over the rough grass – all of this
is that we do, quite within acceptance
      and not to press
      the warm alarm
      but a light
      surface, a day
      lifted from high
      thick roots, upwards.
Where we go is a loved side of the temple,
a place for repose, a concrete path.
There's no mystic moment involved: just
      that we are
      is how, each
      severally, we're
      carried into
the wind which makes no decision and is
a tide, not taken. I saw it
      and love is
      when, how &
      because we
      do: you
could call it Ierusalem or feel it
as you walk, even quite jauntily, over the grass.

The *holy city* is an image of human relationships which, like bodies in a dance, syllables in a stanza, are constantly changing. The poem which embodies it could be two shaken up-sonnets stuck together (as the poem is about a connection being made between two people): fourteen lines up from the central line, fourteen lines down. You can feel your way into it by tracing three inter-linking journeys.

One: follow the verbs. They begin active (*Come up; walks; we go*). Verbs and movement stop at the centre, a place for repose. The next is passive (*carried*). Then acts are done (or not) not by *we* but other things, *wind* and *tide*. After *Ierusalem*, movement starts again, but now it is not *we* who *walk* but *you*, the pronoun which began the poem stationary (*you stand*), as if the poem's achievement is to get *you* going. Something has moved forward. We got to some centre, rested, then went on.

Second journey: follow what happens to *we*. This begins at *we do*; then comes *we go*. After *repose* comes *we are*, then *we're carried* into the *wind* and *tide* of no decision. The climax of this journey is what *love is: when, how & / because we / do.* This journey is edging *we* closer to *love*.

Three, track what happens to the physical: bodies, warmth, *wind, grass*. The poem opens with an imperative, *Come up to it*, i.e. (perhaps) "face it". Face the fact *that the wind is quite warm on the sides / of the face*. Are we talking attraction, a blush, sensual feeling between *you* and the speaker, facing the fact *that it is so*, that this feeling *is felt / as a matter of practice*? Someone is "practised" in reading signs of attraction; but seems *not to agree*: maybe the other is unpractised, maybe it still feels open as to whether attraction is "agreed" to exist. Either way, there are bodies as well as minds involved. Hence *walk* is what we *do*. This is *within acceptance*. (Is this *within* one or other person's acceptance? Or social acceptance?) The outward signs of whatever is *felt* are socially unremarkable but inside is wilder and warmer? On the *light surface* all is casual and gentle; underneath is momentous, sensual, all *thick roots* and lifting *upwards*.

So in this journey, the first half increasingly suggests sensual assent. Then comes *where we go*. As in *holy* of the title, the syllable at the poem's heart is a long O (*go, repose, no, moment*), like a gasp of delight, as we are at rest on a *loved side of the temple*. Embracing, perhaps? This is where *love* comes in. And *Ierusalem*, the archetypal *holy city*.

The poem began with one imperative (*Come*) followed by *as you stand*. It closes with another (*feel*) followed by *as you walk*. Under the reader's nose, bodies have registered each other, moved together. Warmth and *love* have occurred. Now *you* walk on again: *jauntily*. The bodily journey suggests a movement not only forward, but towards and into each other, like the poem's own margins.

The point of this poem is not knowing precisely what happened: being able to keep everything open-ended, all possibilities in play. But if you put the physical journey together with the other two (of the verbs, of *we*) you get an erotic journey, brushed with butterfly lightness. Two bodies and sensibilities moving together, staying still a moment in a sacred central place (*love*), then moving on again in the outside world. A dance which discloses, but never completely.

Moniza Alvi's poem, 'How the World Split in Two', does the opposite. It is crystal clear about what has happened, but does not say what that is. It is all image. Its journeys are minute syllabic echoes. But the subject, the opposite of all three other modern poems I've discussed, is the breaking, not the making, of connection.

It introduces a sequence in which people born in Britain whose parents were immigrant experience racism and fantasize about where they came from. (Alvi, born in Pakistan, grew up in Hertfordshire.) But it is about the transformation of their and everyone's lives by 9/11.

How The World Split In Two

Was it widthways or lengthways,
a quarrel with the equator?
Did the rawness of the inside sparkle?

Only this is true:
there was an arm on one side
and a hand on the other,
a thought on one side
and a hush on the other.

And a luminous tear
carried on the back of a beetle
went backwards and forwards
from one side to the other.

(from *How The Stone Found Its Voice*, Bloodaxe, 2005)

This is a creation myth for the post 9/11 world. Like many creation myths, it gives a small animal the lone heroic task of shouldering the burden of mourning (*carried on the back*), and connecting different sides of the once single *world* through their grief.

Each chunk has its own inner echoes. The first line's repeated AY (*widthways, lengthways*) leads up to *equator*, and repeats the W in that key word of the title: *world was, widthways, lengthways*, a sound the second line repeats in *quarrel* and (again) *equator*. In the third line, *sparkle* picks up *quarrel*, the OR of *rawness* picks up the stressed *Was* at the beginning, and *Did* echoes *widthways* and *with*.

The second chunk ends with a rhyme to the title (*two/true*), showing how important the new *two* is. Then begin mirrorings internal to this chunk: repeats of *on one side, on one side* and *on the other, on the other*; *hush* adds to the short U of *one, one, other, other*. But these syllables also announce their relationships to the first chunk by back-echoes. *Arm* reflects the AR of *sparkle; side and side* pick up *inside; other and other* echo *equator*; the OR of *thought* picks up *rawness*.

The third chunk harmonizes *luminous* with *true*, while *tear* suggests a soft relation with the last syllable of *equator, other, other. Beetle* echoes *quarrel* and *sparkle*; the Ws of *went backwards, forwards* (and repeated in the last line's *one*) remember the Ws of the first two lines (and those of *one, one* in the second chunk). *One side to the other* echoes the repeated pattern in end-words of the second chunk (*one side/ other/ one side/ other*). The OR of *forwards* picks up both *thought* and *rawness* but the one echo internal to this verse alone (*backwards/ back*) adds to the grief imaged by that *tear*. The *world* has been *split* into *one side* and the *other*. It can never go *back*. The poem is about split, but it works, like the other poems, like all good poems, through connection. Above all, of syllables.

"All I know is what the words know"

Olson said syllables come from the mind, the line from the breath and heart, But that's just whimsy. He knew he was being arbitrary. (He called it "didactic".) What does it matter where they come from? What matters is what they do. And getting syllables to belong to each other so ear and mind can be satisfied. So readers, even if they don't understand at once, can trust the words, feel they belong together, and say with Beckett's vagrant in *Molloy*, "All I know is what the words know".

Taken from Ruth Padel's keynote lecture, delivered 18 March 2006 at the conference *Metre and Versification – the State of Play*, in Magdalene College Cambridge, as part of its Year in Literature Festival.

Poetry Review is grateful to the following publishers, poets and their estates for permission to reproduce the poems as follows:
Arc Publications: Julia Darling, 'Two Lighthouses' from *Apology for Absence* (2005)
Bloodaxe Books: Moniza Alvi, 'How the World Split in Two' from *How The Stone Found Its Voice* (2005) and J.H. Prynne, 'The Holy City' from *Poems* (1999)
R.S. Thomas's 'Blackbird', which first appeared in *Agenda* 36:2 (1998) p.7.

REVIEWS

As any courteous egotist knows, the art of shutting-up goes hand in glove with making attention-seeking confessions, then sitting back and watching everybody's faces...
　　—David Morley

Bucketful By Glistering Bucketful

Seamus Heaney, *District and Circle*, Faber, £12.99, ISBN 9870571230969

Heaney's previous two collections, *The Spirit Level* (1996) and, especially, *Electric Light* (2001), were risky and uneven affairs. Lacking the dominating and shaping ritual of his best books, *North*, *Station Island*, and *Seeing Things* (still his masterwork), they often went for a luxuriance of language, and a reach or up-lift which was awkwardly achieved, even when warranted. The wryness had come to feel mannered, the sense of election to the learned fellowship of poets too often untrammelled and untroubled to avoid *our* sense of embarrassment. Re-read now, these most recent books fracture into a small set of achieved lyric one-offs amid an over-riding lack of direction and coherence.

District and Circle represents work consistently higher in achievement, and different in kind, largely because it makes riskiness and venturesomeness into its own procedures. This book sees such uncertainty as part of the general and traumatically conflictual condition of the world across Heaney's lifetime, from the Second World War through to last summer. It also wears its riskiness openly in other ways, right from the page dedicating the book to Heaney's early patron Ann Saddlemyer, which bears an epigraph beginning *"Call her Augusta / Because we arrived in August…"*. Saddlemyer, early provider of the Heaneys' Glanmore cottage, is here set up as the mistress of a latter-day Coole Park. Heaney, exulted (condemned?) by Robert Lowell to be the "best Irish poet since Yeats", again broaches and dares a subject which might prove cringe-worthy for his supporters. At Heaney's current age, Yeats was producing the work that would be gathered in *The Winding Stair and Other Poems*: a book which includes the Coole Park poems, alongside poems on love from old age, and sequences containing the troubling adoption of the voices of women young and old. What is also signalled in the epigraph to *District and Circle*, however, is that Heaney's self-mythologising and vocalisations will be of a different nature; the 'happenstance' of *"Augusta / Because we arrived in August"*, and the fact that the *"bounty"* which August brings is that of *"baled hay and blackberries and combines"*, rather than the model of civic, literary or philosophic order Coole's bounty came to be for Yeats.

The book is a very self-conscious re-visioning of the favoured Heaney themes, however, in a retrospective vein familiar from Yeats's late style.

Poems on farm instruments – a turnip-snedder and harrow-pin appear here – ; undergrounds of various kinds, as the Tube and also as Hades; the Tollund man revives in this late springtime; brick-laying; funerals; the early death of Heaney's brother; his young married life: all are reviewed. But unlike the lustfulness and prurience of Yeats's sense of renewed fertility in this phase, Heaney's is a calm, post-wintering-out exuberance at the return of possibility and fruition, even in age and against continuingly-intransigent circumstance.

The reason for this is formal. Against what seems already to have become a tag-line for the collection, the declaration that 'Anything Can Happen' in its version from Horace there, this is a return by Heaney to a concerted deployment of form and formal variation. Despite his early reputation as a poet able to mirror nature or to evoke the sensuous and physical qualities of objects, it has always been noticeable that Heaney's collections have gathered their force through the adoption of a specific formal model. Think of the "drill-bit" thin quatrains which sustained him through *Wintering Out* and *North* to *Field Work*; the sonnets from this last which reappear in *The Haw Lantern*; the twelve-line 'Squarings' from *Seeing Things* which recur in various combinations ('Squarings' squared) in *The Spirit Level*; the Derek-Mahon-like rhymed quatrains from *Seeing Things* which crop up in *Electric Light*, and again here. But the formal gravity of *District and Circle* is firmly centred upon the sonnet, variously rhymed or unrhymed; a surprising way of abbreviating, managing, and establishing a vast range of personal and impersonal content.

'Anything Can Happen' is freighted by awful historical and global premonition. The sense that at any moment things can randomly shift their ground. And yet what is noticeable also about the book is that it is absolutely assured in its own voice and "stance" – a key word – or the (etymologically-unrelated) way in which the people in the poems take their stand against troubling experience. In 'The Aerodrome', for instance, remembering having become unsettled by watching the wartime planes in 1944 with a young girlfriend, the speaker reflects that love is "dug heels and distance[...] a stance". Describing the way "you had to stand" to swing a sledge-hammer in 'The Shiver', the question raised of the experience is, "did it do you good?" And the answer implied, "of course". The title sonnet sequence, recounting journeys on the London Underground under various kinds of surveillance, its tunnels "flicker-lit", has the speaker recall how:

> On to the carriage metal, I reached to grab
> The stubby black roof-wort and take my stand
> From planted ball of heel to heel of hand

As sweet traction and heavy down-slump swayed me.

To the extent that this speaker, like late Yeats, feels himself to be "the only relict / Of all that I belonged to", he remains like the earlier refugee in 'Exposure' from *North*, someone "escaped from the massacre", whatever grimly recurrent local or global catastrophe that might be.

To this extent, the risk of *District and Circle* is also its command. More assuredly than in *Electric Light*, with its gauche versions of eclogues, this is a book by a pastoral poet once again convinced in his knowledge that the pastoral tradition from Virgil onwards, whilst not immune from echoes of historical carnage, ultimately offers a stance against them. A tactful celebration of the fruits of age, 'The Birch Grove', has a half-mocked, half-recognisable, al fresco breakfaster "dandle a sandal", and declare that "If art teaches us anything[...] it's that the human condition is private." Unstomachable to some, as a response inadequate to its situations and to the vast historical moment or moments raised, this ideal is the challenge which the book offers. The metaphors of blood, and blood itself, flow here, as they did for Yeats at Coole. But the upshot is always a contained and benignant acceptance and possibility, the startling burst of poetry from the "raw sliced mess", as at the end of 'The Turnip-Snedder', emerging "bucketful by glistering bucketful".

Steven Matthews's latest book is *Modernism*, in the Arnold Context Series of which he is General Editor.

☙

Liaisons, Mirrors, Selves

DAVID MORLEY

Hugo Williams, *Collected Poems*, Faber, £14.99, ISBN 0571216919;
Hugo Williams, *Dear Room*, Faber, £8.99, ISBN 0571230377

Osip Mandelshtam, writing his great nonfictional prose account *Journey to Armenia*, wryly supposed, "It must be the greatest impertinence to speak with the reader about the present in that tone of absolute courtesy that we have for some reason yielded to the memoirists". This statement could stand as a working description of how Hugo Williams's poems perform their confident and sometimes dangerous liaisons with readers. His voice is utterly direct; it flatters in its clarity; and it flirts quite openly with their expectations. The impertinence is the poetry's assumed and apparent candour, yet this is deflected by a writerly charm – an apologetic assurednesses, and that absolute courtesy of not letting poems go on too long:

> Ten, no, five seconds
> after coming all
> over the place
> too soon,
>
> I was lying there
> wondering
> where to put the
> line-breaks in.

('Poetry')

As any courteous egotist knows, the art of shutting-up goes hand in glove with making attention-seeking confessions, then sitting back and watching everybody's faces; but then, as any moralist will tell you, confession is the true face of self-deception. A born storyteller (and, yes, a moralist), Williams confesses elegantly, even eagerly on occasion, especially concerning sex. He avoids clichés of feeling; there is no speck of sentimentality or kitsch in what he writes. That does not mean he does not lie; honesty, for a writer, is a literary strategy. Like a rueful Vicomte de Valmont, the moments of his truth sometimes sound like expert shamming, part of a male game plan, yet even his false notes are charming, for they are an intentional part of the liaison between writer and reader:

> When she answered the door
> in her low-cut dress
> I forgot what it was
> I was going to do to her.
> I gave her a kiss
> and asked if she was ready to go out,
> checking my smile
> in the mirror in the hall
> against my chances of being liked.

('My Chances')

So important is the mirror as a motif in his work, Faber could have had a real one as the book's cover. But this is all a pose by someone who likes himself too much and hates himself for liking himself too little. You never entirely trust him (whoever "he" is) despite the lulling humour, the deprecations and undercutting. Yet isn't that his aim? It protects the poems from responsibility, and it keeps you reading, curious to see what the character "Hugo Williams" will be up to next, a process perfected in his excellent prose book *Freelancing*, a study in the dark science of literary survival.

There are two "Hugo"s. One is an actor (from a theatrical dynasty) who performs his life's role through poetry; and the other is a slightly pained observer of the first, who is sometimes fiercely judgmental of that self. They sometimes coexist in the same poem, staring at the other from each side of its mirror; but the first self has taken more of a hammering since *Self-Portrait with a Slide* (1990). This seems to be because, when something seriously serious – death, usually – strikes, all charm is jolted into truth, and the actor-self can't or won't wing it anymore.

At those moments in this *Collected Poems*, you begin to realize you may not trust the first character but you do begin to warm to the second. Thrown out of pose, out of character, as in 'Death of an Actor' (the fine poem sequence to his father's memory), the poetry hits the reader far harder. You get the feeling that writing such a poem hits the poet too; maybe even to the point of making him question himself into a new style. This harder reality has a stammer. It no longer suavely and unfeelingly puts "the / line-breaks in":

> Now that it is late
> Now that it is too late
> For filial piety
> I can but thank him for
> His bloody-mindedness.

Face expressionless with pain
He ordered me a suit in Savile Row
The very day he took
The last plunge backwards
Into secrecy and sweat.
'O Dad, can dead men swim?'

Reading his work on an industrial scale, I got to believing it is not charm or the famous "direct style" that makes Williams persuasive. It is ruthlessness, a completely cold eye for detail and for the pointlessness of things and events. Hugo Williams, like Larkin, is finely tuned to his own purposelessness, but that is his grace, not his curse. In 'During an Absence' for example:

Now that she has left the room for a moment
to powder her nose
we watch and wait, watch and wait
for her to bring back the purpose into our lives.

Williams is not alienated from himself in these poems, unlike many poets who parade their lives in dislocation. He is never self-important enough to assume that his particular life's events are somehow general or mythic. In fact, he makes a point of exploding his importance and even presenting himself as silly. I'd argue that Hugo Williams is blessed by self-awareness, and is neither misanthropic nor whining. He may show contempt for himself on occasion; but never for the reader for whom he takes pains to be clear and open. That demonstrates as much generosity as it does cunning.

Dear Room is a fine collection in which the two "Hugo"s once more slip and slide around each other in imaginary and real spaces. There is no sense of extended territory (as there was in *Writing Home*, say) but a continuation of poetic diplomacy between his selves and their worlds. What gives *Dear Room* gravitas and depth are the poems I assume are written in memory of his sister, the actor Polly Williams. We turn to Hugo Williams for his delightful expertise in tone and, when he is moved by tragedy beyond his control, when he is touched to write completely outside those selves of his, his tone is perfect and a courtesy to true feeling.

David Morley's next collection of poetry is *The Invisible Kings* (Carcanet Press, 2007).

ℬ

No Full Stop

JOHN MCAULIFFE

Michael Donaghy, *Safest*, Picador, £12.99, ISBN 0330440519

Michael Donaghy's poems are often in two minds: serious and comic, direct and sly, allusive and idiomatic. Most of all, they draw attention to their artificiality: even as Donaghy prided himself on defending that artifice and its meaningfulness. His last, posthumous, collection *Safest* is divided into four thematically-coherent sections. But it is united by his interest in these dualities and, throughout, cleaves to one of his art's most basic premises, that poems exist beyond time and beyond their makers. This is a subject on which *Safest* is as brilliantly inventive as his three previous collections.

The book's first poem, 'Upon a Claude Mirror', is a sonnet whose title and opening lines seem remote in vocabulary and tone:

> A lady might pretend to fix her face,
> but scan the room inside her compact mirror –
>
> so gentlemen would scrutinize this glass
> to gaze on Windermere or Rydal Water

It continues, picking up pace and rhyming more emphatically, to switch between the natural scenes of Wordsworth's Lake District and a more rhetorical consideration of the "glass" or "box" or "mirror", those devices for mediating the world:

> and pick their way along the clifftop tracks
> intent upon the romance in the box,
>
> keeping unframed nature at their backs,
> and some would come to grief upon the rocks.

Where Wordsworth, in his less obviously mediated descriptions of Windermere and Rydal Water, reflects and speaks plainly about the spots of time associated with these places, Donaghy's technique is more metaphysical. The *volta* of the sonnet, when it comes, takes a turn that will be familiar to his readers, stopping short and addressing us imperatively, driving home its point about the passage of time:

> Don't look so smug. Don't think you're any safer
> as you blunder forward through your years
>
> squinting to recall some fading pleasure,
> or blinded by some private scrim of tears.

The sonnet's final lines are typically affecting and ingenious, though it ends with what looks like a typo:

> I know. My world's encircled by this prop,
> though all my life I've tried to force it shut

The couplet's sense of entrapment and failure is set aside, though, while readers look at the last line's missing rhyme until we mouth the missing punctuation mark, that absent full stop.

Donaghy's pre-occupation with time and memory, and with poetic form, dominates the book's first section. 'The Apparatus', a disillusioned re-write of Yeats's *Byzantium*, is uneasy in the inhuman, timeless world of objects, finds love uselessly in "This unopened envelope, / This single empty glove" and ends despairingly:

> Who is my accuser?
> Who keeps watch all afternoon?
>   A glass eye, in a locked drawer,
> In a forgotten room.

The little parables of 'Hazards' are lighter, including the great punchline "What part of Noh do you not understand?" although the poem's opening is characteristically provocative:

> Once upon a time there was a dark blue suit.
> And one fine morning the chamberlain laid it out upon a bed
> And the ministers of state assembled round it singing
> *God preserve and protect the emperor!*

The first section's final poem, 'A Darkroom', is a dramatic monologue in the same, influential mode that Donaghy has used in each of his previous books; resembling Ian McEwan and Kazuo Ishiguro as much as Robert Browning and Richard Wilbur in its contrivances. This compressed period narrative reads like a short story while also sustaining a more symbolic or metaphysical reading: here the narrator introduces us to Klein, a photographer and Holocaust survivor, remembered by the narrator in the hellish "red dark" of the darkroom where he shows photographs of his "mother and five sisters / burning back from nothing, fixing them". The next line reads: "I want to come back to this now and again" and the poem exerts fierce pressure on that last phrase until, at the end of the piece, the narrator finds himself "now" (and forever) trapped with Klein, "and the door slammed shut behind me".

There are further narratives and dramatic monologues in sections two and three, which dwell in similar ways on imagined histories and imagined futures, describing a 1960s Weather Underground safe house, the Elizabethan theatre and Hector's death in *The Iliad*. There are also two intriguingly baggy poems, one of which, 'Grimoire' (a "manual of black magic", says the *OED*), goes over the same ground as Donaghy's engaging critical handbook, *Wallflowers*. The other is a fragment from a resumed consideration of the Irish-American Chicago police chief Francis O'Neill, who was the subject of the wonderful sequence 'O'Ryan's Belt' in *Errata*. The fragments here, though, are reminiscent of another early poem, his parody of bardic poems in 'Seven Poems from the Welsh' in *Shibboleth*, with their sudden pratfalls as when the song of the (mythical) first Irish poet Amergin deteriorates into:

> I am the foam on the wave
> I am the bright wave on the white sand
> I am a foredeck gorilla
> I am a lost shoe at a crossroads dance
> if anyone asks

The book's last, longest section includes five 'Akhmatova Variations' – which apply Donaghy's technique to a subject and sound quite different from that of the rest of the book – but this final section is chiefly comprised of poems which picture the poet and his family, or rather place them within the same mortal and immortalising imagination that defines each of the other sections. There are poems about funerals and illness which now seem doubly moving; a lovely lullaby; a poem that freezes his father in an endless game of chess. There are also two sonnets that re-write Wordsworth's Westminster Bridge in very different ways. The first, 'Midriver', stops time, the speaker and the poem mid-bridge. Its first line highlights the compressed visual wit of Donaghy's technique, where the hyphen stands in for a bridge, and then spatialises time so that the future and the past become two "then"s on either bank of the Thames:

– and is a bridge: Now to either then:

The next poem, 'The River Glideth Of His Own Sweet Will', sets that mid-bridge speaker in motion although now it turns out that he is a younger self, a "buck of eighteen", oblivious to the hospitalized man (his older self?) "wired up to a heart monitor / staring north to Big Ben's crackled face". Another sonnet, 'Southwesternmost', looks in an entirely different direction though it is just as profoundly concerned with time as it remembers Donaghy's Kerry mother:

I've a pocketwatch for telling space,
a compass tooled for reckoning by time,
to search this quadrant between six and nine
for traces of her song, her scent, her face.
Come night, that we might seek her there, come soon,
come shade the southwest quarter of this chart,
the damaged chamber of my mother's heart.

This touching poem's "pocketwatch for telling space" would be a useful instrument to measure *Safest*'s effect. That is: *Safest* looks short, its index lists only twenty-four titles, yet it reads, satisfyingly, like a much longer book. Across this and indeed all four of his collections, Donaghy's poems are characterized by an artful, serious skepticism and an utterly distinctive density and music. They look already like one of this era's lasting and defining pleasures.

John McAuliffe's first collection is *A Better Life* (Gallery). He teaches creative writing at the University of Manchester.

☙

Amongst Wreckage And Light

MATTHEW JARVIS

John Burnside, *Selected Poems*, Cape, £12, ISBN 0224078038;
John Burnside, *A Lie About My Father*, Cape, £12.99, ISBN 0224074873

John Burnside's *Selected Poems* draws its contents from eight of the nine individual collections of poetry he has produced to date. Its poetic is characterised by a slowly growing scope, but also by a distinctly sustained sensibility – a sense of poetry as meditation, as a space for the quiet contemplation of things in the world. This is apparent from early on in the volume (which is usefully arranged chronologically, by collection), in the poem 'Halloween', in which the speaker is marked out precisely as one who observes:

> I have learned to observe the winters:
> the apples that fall for days
> in abandoned yards,
> the fernwork of ice and water
> sealing me up with the dead
> in misted rooms
>
> as I come to define my place:
> barn owls hunting in pairs along the hedge,
> the smell of frost on the linen, the smell of leaves
> and the whiteness that breeds in the flaked
> leaf mould [...]

What is important here is the way in which the poetic eye takes time to accumulate detail, to dwell upon the minutiae of the world – apples in "abandoned yards", frost on linen – to form a slow, accretive rendition of the poem's larger objects of attention ("winters", "my place").

In later pieces, such dwelling *upon* the world becomes a way of exploring what it means to be dwelling *in* the world. For example, 'Ports' – one of a number of superb longer poems drawn from the justly lauded collection *The Asylum Dance* – reflects on the notion of 'home':

> Whenever we think of home
> we come to this:

the handful of birds and plants we know by name
rain on the fishmonger's window
                              the walleyed plaice
freckled with spots
                    the colour of orangeade.

We look for the sifted light
that settles around the salvaged
hull of the *Research*
                    perched on its metal stocks
by the harbour wall.

Home, 'Haven', "Our dwelling place" is a matter of accumulated detail, of objects brought together under poetry's meditative scrutiny. For Burnside's poetic, in other words, being in the world is a matter of attention to what is, as the same poem puts it, "shifting around you / endlessly // entwined". However, as the conclusion to 'Ports' indicates, dwelling is not at all passive; rather, it is crucially to do with choosing objects through which the process of being in the world may be pursued. Thus, observing a boat called 'Serenity', the speaker notes:

In daylight it would seem
almost absurd:
too sentimental
              gauche
                    inaccurate
a weekend sailor's image of the sea

but now [...]
          it is only what it seems:

a name for something wanted
                    and believed

no more or less correct than anything
we use to make a dwelling in the world.

Dwelling, in short, is a matter of active construction – of choosing those things that will best serve what is "wanted / and believed".

Much of Burnside's poetry here is bound up with the issue of being in the world, but other concerns are manifest too. For example, there is a recurrent interest in being lost or vanishing. Thus, in one early piece, the poet-persona is "lost on purpose", as he searches for "the lithe / weasel in the grass" ('Lost'). Similarly, the later poem, 'Roads', suggests the desire simply to fade away:

> I wanted to stop the car and disappear
> to pull in under a cypress and slip away
> venturing into the nowhere
> of starlight and wind
> and leaving no trace.

However, disappearance is not something Burnside's poetry necessarily celebrates. In 'History', for example, it is contemplated with horror:

> Sometimes I am dizzy with the fear
> of losing everything – the sea, the sky,
> all living creatures, forests, estuaries

This poem is apparently responding to the events of September 11th 2001. But the fear of loss generated by "the news in my mind, and the muffled dread / of what may come" transmutes, at this point, into a striking environmental consciousness. The challenge, as Burnside puts it towards the end of the poem, thus becomes "how to be alive / in all this gazed-upon and cherished world / and do no harm".

Such a conclusion is, perhaps, unsurprising, given what is revealed in Burnside's memoir, *A Lie About My Father*. This book is, in large part, precisely about the harm done by people to one another – in this case, the harm done by the writer's alcoholic, abusive father to his family. Thus, in the book's short opening section ('Birdland'), having been asked about his father by a hitch-hiker he has picked up, Burnside observes:

> I could have told Mike the truth. I could have talked about the
> violence, the drinking, the shameful, maudlin theatre of his
> penitences. I could have told him about the gambling, and the
> fits of manic destruction. I could have spoken for hours about
> his cruelty, his pettiness, the way he picked obsessively at
> everything I did when I was too small and fearful to defend
> myself.

The book undoubtedly fulfils the grim pictures that this initial sketch suggests. It is a memoir of psychological tortures exacted on a small boy by someone for whom "cruelty was an ideology"; it is a record of profound failure, in a father's "perennial dissatisfaction with his lot" and in the way he persistently destroys his family's hopes; and it is a witness to violence – although Burnside carefully gives little detail of this, preferring understated comments such as "At home, my father was often ugly and violent", and thus steering well clear of melodrama. Moreover, the book also charts Burnside's own extended psychological collapse, which results in two periods of residence in a psychiatric institution. In short, this is never comfortable reading.

It is, however, often beautifully rendered. Admittedly, I could do without the overt fictionalising of certain identities in phrases like "I'm going to call him Mike" or "I'll call her Sandra Fulton"; I also think that occasional remarks come dangerously close to weak generalisation ("men and women love for different reasons"). However, the prose achieves a glorious lyricism. Thus, when Corby public library is burnt down one winter, Burnside stands amongst its ruins, looking at the "remnants of burned books":

> By that time, a book was the closest thing to holy that I knew,
> but I couldn't deny the frisson of pleasure I experienced,
> seeing those ashes – those words, those ideas, the foreign
> beauty of those texts – melting away in the snow.

In such passages, Burnside's prose approaches the striking poise of his poetry, creating shafts of clear light amidst the harsh subject-matter that characterises much of his memoir. Indeed, as one of his poems suggests, it is precisely this combination that constitutes – within what is becoming a significant literary vision – the business of being in the world. For this, writes Burnside in 'Ports', is "our / dwelling place: / a catalogue of wrecks / and slants of light".

Matthew Jarvis is currently writing a book called *Place and Environment in Radical British Poetry* (for Rodopi).

☙

Heart-sick Wonder

TIM LIARDET

Robin Robertson, *Swithering*, Cape, £8.99, ISBN 033044168X

Perhaps all poets manifest some knowledge of the existential loneliness required to generate their work. But few can be better than Robin Robertson at giving new names to its separating elements, its simultaneous advantages and disadvantages. There cannot be many poets who understand so well how bound-up this state is with the evolution of identity. That knowledge, infused as it is with spiritualised longing, has led him to write the most rueful, melancholic and numinously painful poems I have read in a very long time. Yet the sombre chimes with the affirmative: Robertson is always acutely aware how world-wonder and passionate endeavour balance the costs of apartness: "…all this life and all its heart-sick wonder / is just the following of a wall / ridged with bright shards of broken glass."

Nature figures strongly here. Often there is a sort of wilful Lawrentian stepping out into the wilderness, away from warmth and comfort; and with some ambivalence as to which way the narrator would rather be heading – like his updated Actaeon, "torn between running home to the palace, / or hiding out here in the woods." Having brought his small daughter back to the warm house, in 'Leavings', the father turns back into the snow:

> I step back out, and see where my footprints turn
> and walk through hers,
> the other way – following the trail
> of rabbit and deer into the unreachable silences of snow.

Earlier, in 'To My Daughters, Asleep', the same father laments that "I see my daughters growing away from me," and – perhaps most touchingly – when his daughter runs through the shallows in 'Donegal' the father is left with his hands full of clothes, full of "all the years"; and can only witness "his daughter going / where he knew he could not follow." There is much walking away; and, if it's possible, the boots face both ways at once. Walking away becomes a walking *towards* that state of sufficiency Robertson knows must be kept inviolable, intact. Balancing this is his simultaneous lament for the manner in which that leaves his relationship to others forever stuck in another key. Indeed, layers of ambivalence course through this book, leading Robertson to the Scottish verb to *swither*: to be uncertain as to which course of action to choose.

The almost-incidental masterpiece of this collection (and there are several candidates) is probably 'Manifest'. The poem is a stunning act of witness, nothing less than Robertson's confrontation of the battered, ruminant facts of embodiment: the trace of morphine in the nails, the blood-string in the stools, the bowel's gleet, the "signatures of taint and septicaemia" all balanced there with irony and devastating ruefulness:

> Try to construct me from the heraldry of the flesh,
> the thick blur of scar tissue, shreds of clothing,
> the burst vessel in the eye like a twist in a marble,
> those frost-feather wrinkles at the side of the mouth[…]
> Shall I tell you? Shall I tell you the secret? *My whole life.*

The companion piece to this poem, for me, is 'Entropy' where the speaker considers a presumably-godless urban reality: "Not praying, just shielding my eyes from the glare […] / not praying, just on my knees in the dark." It is this kind of quasi-hieratic experience, full of a sort of divine itch, which may have triggered Robertson's fascination with Strindberg in two poems here. The first is set in London, where Strindberg endured an unhappy honeymoon with his second wife, "Dragged through other peoples' lives, / pursued through my own"; the next in Paris, three years later, by which time he has shed his wife and children and is found, in an elegant reworking of the pram-in-the-hall, "…forging lines of gold from lead." Elsewhere, this recognition of the need for separation seems to lead Robertson quite naturally to another species of artistic priesthood; a Hughesian respect for otherness in nature. In horses, 'The Eel', 'Lizard', 'Trumpeter Swan' and, most strikingly, the hawk that takes to flight "unmade, unmanned," he finds the image of his own flawed sufficiency.

Such themes are extended further through Robertson's re-workings of Ovid. 'The Death of Actaeon' slyly debunks and sabotages the original as it explores the way in which an enchanted landscape succumbs to "the whole pack, thick with bloodlust"; and seems almost to burst at the seams with a sense of unfulfillable longing. 'Actaeon: The Early Years', the sixteen apparently-autobiographical vignettes which spin out a narrative over some five pages of relaxed sextets, explore a child's uneasy relationship with a brutalising mother: "Her migraines were his fault, being the wrong child." Within this macabre *danse* the child catches sight of his mother in the bath, is corroded by post-Freudian guilt, gets knocked to the ground and takes refuge in a suitably Ovidian monkey tree where he must first learn how to disappear and then, rather too early, how "desire for intimacy / was a transgression" and fear of intimacy entirely natural:

> Twenty years spent
> edging past a migraine's darkened room. He slipped a note
> into a gap in the floorboards:
> 'all the roads I walk will be away from you.'

This poem might just be *Swithering*'s centre of gravity. Its denouement epitomises the notes profoundly struck in so many of the poems that precede and succeed it.

Achieving unity on this scale requires formidable intellectual and technical control; yet Robinson's devices are never foregrounded, and *Swithering* reveals his discerning eclecticism. In a collection whose shifts in scale are breath-taking, within a consistent intimacy of tone, Robinson shows himself a master as much of tradition as of the actual world, both human and – if there is a distinction to be made – natural.

Tim Liardet's *The Blood Choir* (2006) is a PBS Recommendation.

ॐ

Passionate Profundities

DOUGLAS HOUSTON

Geoffrey Hill, *Without Title*, Penguin Books, £9.99, ISBN 139780141020259;
Jeffrey Wainwright, *Acceptable Words*, £42.75, ISBN 0719067549

Without Title is an uncompromising collection. The title itself gives nothing away, beyond, perhaps, announcing the absence of any clear thematic structure of the kind that has sustained most of Geoffrey Hill's preceding books. In this collection, he has liberated himself into a surprising range and variety of registers, subjects and styles.

The passionate profundities of Hill's historical and religious imagination persist in many of the best poems. His continuing "sombre litigation with the body of language", to quote from the thirteenth of the book's 'Pindarics' sequence, presses his interrogations of poetry, philosophy, and belief to occasional extremes of erudite inaccessibility. Alongside his unyieldingly magisterial manner, however, is heard a less familiar, conversationally direct voice that reflexively qualifies the *gravitas* of his recondite and sometimes acutely personal preoccupations. The closing line of 'On the Reality of the Symbol' – "This is late scaffold-humour, turn me off" – offers an example. It bluntly tells the reader to take it or leave it, while self-deprecatingly acknowledging that age and heightened apprehensions of mortality offer a licence to prioritise the internal imperatives that drive much of *Without Title*.

The poet's intention of forging ahead in their pursuit exposes him, as the eighth of the 'Pindarics' indicates, to the risk of falling short of what he has already achieved:

> I can't do better now than hunt a phrase,
> Old mystic howler clutching at a note.

Hill is, however, no whit deterred from faring forward. His metres and general conceptions of form also display new freedom and flexibility. The iambic pentameter is emphatically present as a basis for much of the verse, but no poem is ever allowed to settle into overall metronomic regularity. Similarly, there is barely a rhymed pair of lines in the book, though its syllabic music can equal in richness the magnificent formality of *In Tenebrae* and much else Hill has produced:

> an unearthed wasps' nest like a paper skull,
> where fragile cauls of cobweb start to shine.
> Where the quick spider mummifies its dead
> Rage shall move somnolent yet unappeased.

('In Ipsley Church Lane 1')

Without Title is equally capable of departing conspicuously from the mandarin traditions that Hill's work has often so forcefully upheld. 'Improvisations for Jimi Hendrix' is as unexpected in its tribute to a perennial hero of pop culture as in its imagery and language. The poem's lines combine disparate elements in a manner that can be so radically disjunctive that William Burroughs's cut-ups come to mind in passages like the following:

> By rights you shall have
> top prize longevity
> wiped as a gift.

Similarly, there are poems in which high culture meets dirty realism the further to confound one's expectations of Hill's work. The fifth part of 'In the Valley of the Arrow' provides an example:

> Unzipped and found addressing the smeared walls
> Of an underpass, crying not my
> Address, no more unnamed accusers,
>
> Self-dubbed natural thespian enacts
> Age, incapacity – judge the witnesses –
> Brings himself off to video'd provocation.

At the shifting centre of *Without Title* is dialogue: dialogue with selfhood and mortality, with contemporary and historical cultural perspectives and with named individuals, both dead and alive. The centre of the book is occupied by the twenty-one poems of twenty-three lines that make up the unremittingly dialogic 'Pindarics' sequence. Here, Hill engages Cesar Pavese as a spectral correspondent and point of orientation in verse of unbridled thematic scope that encompasses the central concerns of this and his other collections. The incessant mobility of this discourse brings to mind the Ezra Pound of the *Cantos*, who, though kept at a moral and aesthetic distance, is repeatedly invoked. Hill's remoteness from a culturally desolate present he must term a "foreign planet" ('Chromatic Tunes') resembles that maintained by Pound throughout everything he wrote after 'Hugh Selwyn Mauberley'. Like the Pound of the *Cantos*, Hill spins out "the skein of talk of my invention" ('Pindarics, 19') with startling inventiveness and energetic freedom of movement throughout the sequence's considerable length. The laminations of theme and meaning that characterise 'Pindarics' demand multiple readings and richly reward the persistent reader. The poems are alive with a mercurial continuity that runs through every line with the immediacy of thought in the process of occurring.

The most accessible and perhaps the finest poems in *Without Title* are vehicles for Hill's profoundly lyrical responses to the natural and physical world. There are a generous number of these. Their luminous particularity of imagery serves as a counter to the book's sometimes unrelentingly cerebral tendencies. Some, like the 'In Ipsley Church Lane' group, 'Offertorium December 2002' and others open onto a dimension of Anglican orthodoxy through the connotations of their titles and the devotional intensity of their focus on transcendental glimpses of the natural world:

> Profoundly silent January shows up

Clamant with colour, greening in fine rain,
Luminous malachite of twig-thicket and bole
Brightest at sundown.

('Epiphany at Hurcott')

The epiphany here is both calendrical and theophanic, the world as the miracle of what is the case.

Without Title sustains the power and grandeur of Hill's *oeuvre* while expanding its scope into new and sometimes challengingly unfamiliar territories. His work over the fifty years since the earliest of his collected poems finds a uniquely responsive critic in Jeffrey Wainwright, whose own poetic exercise of the historical imagination can rival Hill's in authority and dramatic impact. The eleven essays making up Wainwright's *Acceptable Words* examine the complex continuities of Hill's poetry throughout the collections he has published since *For the Unfallen* appeared in 1959.

The essays continually draw attention to the ways in which Hill achieves the resonant sublimities of language that essentially distinguish his work. The opening sentence of the first essay announces that "The first wonder of poetry lies in the immediate effects of language". Above and beyond Wainwright's expert tracings of the epistemological structures of Hill's verse, the essays recurrently and minutely investigate the syllabic and metrical events that make Hill's work primarily memorable for its sheer effects of language. It's refreshing to read these essays that are so uncluttered with the apparatus of theoretical frames of reference and so keenly in touch with the actual fabric of the verse they critically engage and celebrate.

Douglas Houston's latest collection is *The Welsh Book of the Dead* (2003).

ℬ

Dramatic Dialogue

MICHELENE WANDOR

Peter Oswald, *Schiller's Mary Stuart*, Oberon Books, £8.99, ISBN 1840025794;
Simon Armitage, *Homer's Odyssey*, Faber, £4.99, ISBN 9785712293152

The grumpy news first. I'm somewhat bewildered by the cover of the first of these books. Peter Oswald's recasting of Schiller's monumental play hides behind shades of black and grey, evoking some dark, gloomy, perhaps clandestine intrigue. This may be relevant to the play's theme, but it unfortunately also obscures the name of the person to whom we owe this crystalline and sensitive version. Just to stay with grumpy for some time longer, there is also no introductory matter to the play. So, for example, we're not told that 2005 was the 200th anniversary of Schiller's death, or anything about the form or language of the original, first produced in 1800. On the other hand, there is a cast list for the Donmar Warehouse production for which Oswald wrote the play. I didn't see the performances, but my guess is that the combination of Harriet Walter's Elizabeth, Janet McTeer's Mary and Barbara Jefford's role as Mary's maid must have been a powerful one.

The good news now: more than good, in fact. Part of the impetus behind Schiller's play was to imagine an encounter between Elizabeth and Mary, something which, as far as we know, never took place. In fact, they meet only once here: in a scene where nothing is resolved, and where the two face each other as political and personal rivals. The rest of the story revolves round the plotting of various courtiers, and Elizabeth's dilemma: on the one hand, there are times when she wants to abdicate her royal responsibilities, and, on the other, she both refuses to, and cannot, relinquish her power. Because Oswald's rhythmic and direct version alternates the formality of poised iambic lines with easy colloquial phrases, he brings out the more personal aspects of the story: beneath the endlessly interesting political unravellings lurks a rather conventional eternal triangle. The older Elizabeth vies with Mary for Leicester's love, and the confluence of personal-political dilemmas deny Elizabeth any real freedom of choice. Interestingly, the very modernity of Oswald's tone helps to enable an almost proto-feminist reading of a text first written in a very different spirit.

I haven't read the Schiller in the original German, but from my nodding knowledge of Goethe, Oswald's transformation of High German Romantic versification into accessible, readable and yet still formal, English is impressive. One has to judge this kind of translation, in the end, as much on its pleasurable readability and clarity as on its linguistic accuracy.

Simon Armitage has undertaken a more ambitious task. In rendering Homer's *Odyssey* from its original ancient rhetorical style into poetic dialogue, he effects a major transformation without selling the epic story short. Written as a commission for radio, the 'books' are compressed into limpid scenes of spare dialogue, often only between two or three characters. I may have only middling German, but I have even less Greek – none at all, in fact – and my Penguin translation, the excellent classic version by E. V. Rieu, is also one of the versions from which Armitage worked. While Oswald's text is more strictly a translation, Armitage really has mined, culled and transformed his material.

The scenes in this version of the *Odyssey* are clearly and dramatically articulated. They are relatively short, making the repetitive, expositional and retrospectively narrative style of the Greek immediate; and punctuated with the absolute minimum of solo voicing – soliloquy. Almost at the centre of the piece is the one substantial soliloquy from Odysseus, in poem-paragraphs, rhythmically varying formality with the colloquial (for example, an easy interpolation of the word 'palaver').

In this transformation, Armitage does far more than distil and represent. He takes poetic and dramatic licence: for example giving the formidable, carnivorous Cyclops a literal voice. The Cyclops, who speaks in a grammatically-broken English and, when its passions are roused, descends into nonsense-sounds, is characterised as a creature whose *mores* are strange and whose very language is made strange, expressing inexpressible emotions. Meanwhile, because dialogue privileges the voice of the individual, certain figures and relationships are foregrounded throughout. Odysseus leaves his wife, Penelope, and their son, Telemachus, to go on a voyage; and he is away for twenty years. The adventures he has – encounters with shipwreck, witches, the seductive Sirens – all happen in the present tense of dialogue; in this way the original's picaresque drive is shaped into something which renders myths – which are probably less familiar to most people than they once were – more accessible by focussing on fewer characters.

However, Armitage retains the power structure which underpins the Greek mythical imperative. His beginning and end consist of debates between the Gods, with Athena more sympathetic towards the humans than is her husband Zeus. Armitage thus frames the play within a pseudo-democratic Olympic discussion, as challenges and favours are parcelled-out; and this elevated domestic pairing is given a more down-to earth parallel in the parting and reunion of Penelope and Odysseus. In the end, it is this more radical of the two treatments reviewed here which ironically both transforms and returns its original to some of its historical roots. By giving every character/figure in the *Odyssey* his or her own voice, Armitage creates a modern echo of that oral tradition of story-telling which has been superseded in our time by the convention of the novel. Both books, in their different ways, have helped to reinvigorate the pleasures in verse-drama, as readable as it is actable.

Michelene Wandor's *Musica Transalpina* (2006) is a PBS Recommendation

☙

Not Him

ROD MENGHAM

I not I: Nauman, Guston, Beckett, Royal Hibernian Academy, Dublin, 2006

The title of the exhibition now running at the Royal Hibernian Academy in Dublin is *I not I*; which proposes a symmetry non-existent in the Beckett title it is alluding to. The show is organized around filmed versions of three Beckett texts (*Breath, Act Without Words I* and *Not I*) and features both direct responses to Beckett's work and imagined associations with it, in videos and sculptures by Bruce Nauman and canvases by Philip Guston. It may be that the assertive doubling of the first person pronoun is intended to emphasise the curator's desire to find resilience rather than defeat in Beckett's work, even in texts where these qualities and outcomes are held in unbearable tension. The real gamble of this exhibition involves the encircling of three distinct interpretations of Beckett's work with the parallel enquiries of Guston and Nauman in order to "offer some companionship" to the writer's vision.

Companionship, or at least 'company' of some sort, is often hinted at in Beckett's post-war oeuvre, but it is effectively fended off in Neil Jordan's filmed version of *Not I* (2000). Apart from a few seconds at the start of the film, the camera stays glued to a close-up examination of the mouth of the actress Julianne Moore. This makes it impossible for the viewer to be aware of the mysterious "auditor" present in the stage productions. In Beckett's original conception, the mouth was faintly-lit within a large area of surrounding darkness, with none of the rest of the face or body visible. In Jordan's version, the actress walks into view fully lit and sits down in a seat with headrest and armrests that look like they have been designed for restraint. From then on, the focus stays on the bright Hollywood perfection of Moore's lips and gleaming teeth, which form a curious barrier to identification in the experiencing of a text that pivots on questions of identification: suspending it, leading towards it, hesitating it. Beckett's

'Mouth' cannot keep company with herself, but is pushed to the brink of doing so, and the audience is meant to accompany her in this struggle.

Not I and *Act Without Words I* are among Beckett's most Sisyphean works, but on the page they seem to keep in balance the opposing forces of prohibition and resurgence, the reasons for "not going on" and "going on" simultaneously. Karel Reisz's filmed version of *Act Without Words I* (2000) tips the balance in favour of prohibition, converting neutral stage directions into facial expressions of despair and chagrin. Strangely enough, it is in Damien Hirst's account of *Breath* (2000), perhaps the most reductive text in the entire oeuvre, that the spirit of resurgence is reflected. The static point of view of a theatre audience is replaced by the dramatically mobile vector of a camera in orbit over the tableau of rubbish, with at least the suggestion of a diurnal rhythm of renewal.

Of the two artists whose work is juxtaposed with these three versions of Beckett's vision, Nauman is the more direct in his response to the writer's example. The earliest of his films and videos being screened, *Slow Angle Walk* (1968), is actually subtitled *Beckett Walk*. The later compositions, *Good Boy, Bad Boy* (1985) and *Clown Torture* (1987), are much more ambitious in conception, and provide lurid magnifications of typically Beckettian scenarios, but their tone and address are much more brutal and less complicated than anything in Beckett's prose or drama. *Clown Torture* focuses on apparently endless repetitions or prolongations of the same kind of hopeless Sisyphean impasse, without any glimmer of alleviation or any approximation to Beckett's use of humour. This spectacle of endurance is one of several Nauman works in which the experience of the viewer is one of mild torment. With *Good Boy, Bad Boy* the antagonism is pronounced; the address to the audience is full-frontal and increasingly aggressive.

In Beckett's texts, the relationship between speaker and reader or listener is often managed with sarcastic wit, not with splenetic confrontation. Guston's mordancy seems more Beckettian than Nauman's angry futility. His use of cartoon-like figuration has an edge of humour equivalent to Beckett's use of sarcasm to encrypt trauma and catastrophe. Interestingly, the images on display include that of *Aggressor* (1978), which bears a superficial resemblance to Nauman's scenarios of confrontation. However, the two figures in this painting oppose one another literally eyeball to eyeball, with an absurdity that recalls the mirroring, doubling and symbiosis that Beckett renders so poignantly throughout his oeuvre. In the end, it is a closely similar variety of tones, ranging from the deadly to the ludicrous, that Guston and Beckett seem to share; that Nauman's more schematic portrayals of alienation seem powerless to reflect.

Rod Mengham is Reader in Modern English Literature at the University of Cambridge and Curator of Works of Art at Jesus College, Cambridge.

ENDPAPERS

Politics is about as defensive as a dysfunctional writers' workshop.
— Lemn Sissay

LETTER FROM WELLINGTON

BILL MANHIRE

Some of us were a bit bewildered when the American poet Robert Hass, a guest at a recent Wellington writing festival, began quoting New Zealand poems from memory. After all, New Zealand poets expect their work to go unread. Didn't R.A.K. Mason, often called our first real poet, write something called 'Song of Allegiance'? This was a roll-call of the great departed ("Shakespeare Milton Keats are dead / Donne lies in a lowly bed" etc) which ended with an image of Mason himself, toiling stoically at the back of the line, confident of not much more than a lack of audience:

> Though my voice is cracked and harsh
> stoutly in the rear I march
>
> Though my song have none to hear
> boldly bring I up the rear.

Yet there were others who heard Hass in Wellington who seemed entirely unsurprised at what he could summon up from memory. Why wouldn't he know the work of our poets? Isn't our poetry on a roll? Isn't it simply available everywhere?

New Zealand poetry has been changing: especially its sense of what is possible. For various reasons, the last two decades of the twentieth century saw it break decisively away from the single British line it had once toiled along at the back of. Our poets began to look both outwards and inwards with equal vigour, and always with a confidence that riches would be found.

And then along came the internet. If the web has been good for poetry in general, this has been especially so here. Writers no longer have to depend on the old blinkered colonial distribution networks to overcome geographical distance. Magazines like *Sport* and *Landfall* remain important poetry venues, as do anthologies, but they have been joined by on-line magazines and websites like *Best New Zealand Poems* and the *New Zealand Electronic Poetry Centre*.

Best New Zealand Poems (now up to its fifth issue) annually selects twenty-five poems which have appeared in magazines or collections in the preceding year. There are notes by the poets, and links to publishing houses and related information sources. It has become a very busy gateway: over 70% of its visitors are international. *NZEPC* is an even broader undertaking. It has a leaning towards various derivatives of Language poetry, but like *BNZP* it tries to be eclectic in its range. At the time of writing it contains resource pages for thirty poets along with many other features.

Indeed, the variety of recent New Zealand poetry is probably its strongest characteristic. The range is crankier, and the writing often less polished, than you might find in contemporary poetry in Britain. All the energy that once crackled through our national form, the short story, has leapt across to poetry. We have our factions of course, often forms of regional antagonism, but there is also a plentiful supply of mavericks. Some of the invisible poetry mavericks of the past are being recovered, too: Robin Hyde, Janet Frame, Len Lye.

The strongest poetry lists come from the two main university presses (Victoria and Auckland), who also have high production values; but there are plenty of other smaller publishers at work. And there are unlikely and imaginative patrons. A wine company sponsors the biennially-appointed New Zealand poet laureate; a law firm has been funding a nationwide secondary schools' poetry award. New Zealand Post has occasionally been known to rig up its mail-boxes so that, when a letter is posted, a disembodied voice declaims a poem to innocent passers-by. There is a $60,000 Prime Minister's Award in poetry, presented annually by the PM herself (she is also Arts Minister).

If R.A.K. Mason's heroic single line is gone (and probably at the moment there are no individual poets working at the level of the late Allen Curnow), there are nevertheless fifty or sixty people in a population of four million writing very well indeed. This means that, like the current All Blacks, we can probably field several first-class teams, any of which would stand a good chance of knocking over the opposition. A couple of my current favourite poets are Jenny Bornholdt and Anne Kennedy, neither of whom publish outside New Zealand; both can easily be sampled in digital form. And there are new books from – and some of us relish these names – James Brown (*The Year of the Bicycle*) and Michael Jackson (*Dead Reckoning*). Brown is a firmly local poet, who lives in a Wellington suburb whose streets are all named after European rivers. Jackson is a distinguished (presently Harvard) anthropologist who has spent most of his life outside New Zealand. (The New Zealand diaspora is surprisingly extensive, with about a fifth of the population overseas.) But each writer seems equally part of what is going on.

Maori and Pacific Island poets are starting to develop the sort of capacity and sense of adventure that has been there in the work of novelists like Patricia Grace, Keri Hulme, Witi Ihimaera, and Albert Wendt. There is an anthology, *Whetu Moana: Contemporary Polynesian Poems in English* (2003), which is sampled on the *NZEPC* site. A powerful, even more recent voice is Tusiata Avia, whose *Wild Dogs Under My Skirt* has been reprinted within a year of publication.

The book I would myself most love to read would be a set of fresh translations of Maori song-poetry. Much remarkable work is already available in the four-volume *Nga Moteatea* (presently being republished by Auckland University Press), where facing page translations and scholarly notes give us a sense of the power of New Zealand's other poetic tradition. The difficulty for Pakeha readers like me is that *Nga Moteatea*'s English translations, made by remarkable Maori scholars in the mid-20th-century, were dated even when they appeared, and now read like a rich pastiche of the more decorative, pseudo-Elizabethan parts of Victorian verse. *Oh mesdames all, be not importunate with me!* But these translations have become *taonga* (cultural treasures) in their own right, and it will be a brave person, Maori or Pakeha, who attempts to replace them.

Best New Zealand Poems
http://www.vuw.ac.nz/modernletters/bnzp/
New Zealand Electronic Poetry Centre
http://www.nzepc.auckland.ac.nz/

Bill Manhire's poems can be found on pp. 23-4

EDITORIAL

Summertime is, *Poetry Review* hopes, a time for slacking: for shaking the spiders out of the hammock, lying back and thinking of poetry. In this issue, the pleasure principle is to the fore as we celebrate Fleur Adcock's receipt of the Queen's Gold Medal and publish a "Letter from Wellington" by her distinguished compatriot Bill Manhire. The first poet-in-residence of Antartica, his is one of those poetries – like that of Hawaii's most lucid shaman, William Merwin; or our own poets from John Burnside to the surprising Tiffany Atkinson – which, while it seduces and subverts the ear, does so partly in order to convey a straight-forward message about the importance of attention.

Such attention is ecological, personal and poetic. And attention emerged as a theme from the May launch of *Free Verse*, Spread the Word's report on publishing opportunities for Black and Ethnic Minority writers, at London's South Bank. It is not the role of an editor to *police* the writing of groups to which she doesn't belong; but to *explore* it. This means not making assumptions, reading from a template that may be partial, or out-of-date, or – worse – tendentious. It's the hardest of editorial disciplines. Having opinions, taste, "standards" and critical authority are easy enough. Listening is harder (as years of community practice certainly taught this editor). And – if as is the case with current *PR* practice – this sometimes results in the paradox of statistical "*over*-representation", the rewards in terms of variety, range and the "shock of the new" (always problematic in British culture) are nevertheless correspondingly increased.

As Lemn Sissay's new occasional column 'News from the Beat' shows, such entente is neither automatic not straightforward. So we're glad to contextualise more familiar Caribbean writing in English by publishing a taster of Francophone Caribbean verse in collaboration with Europe's oldest poetry festival, the Struga Poetry Evenings. Elsewhere, we continue the festive range with festival keynotes from both Ruth Padel and Michael Schmidt; feature a specially-commissioned cover by one of Austria's leading artists, Johann Julian Taupe; enquire after the origins of Elaine Feinstein's writerly art; and join a poetry conversation on the art of travelling gracefully. Welcome aboard.

FIONA SAMPSON

Fleur Adcock Wins The Queen's Gold Medal for Poetry

Poetry Review congratulates Fleur Adcock, the seventh woman recipient of the Queens's Gold Medal for Poetry. Instigated in 1933, the award became open to Commonwealth as well as British citizens in 1985. Recommendations are made by a committee chaired by the Poet Laureate; and the announcement is made on Shakespeare's birthday, April 23rd. New Zealander Adcock, who settled permanently in the UK in 1963, receives the Medal for her collected *Poems 1960-2000*. She has also received an OBE (1996); and was made a Fellow of the Royal Society of Literature in 1984. As well as publishing ten collections of poetry, Adcock has edited a number of influential anthologies, including *The Faber Book of Twentieth Century Women's Poetry* (1987).

Fast Forward

Holding the photograph of Mary Ellen,
my great-grandmother the midwife,
to gaze more closely at her face,
I see on my desk behind the frame
another picture, in another frame:
my blonde granddaughter holding her baby.
They are standing in a doorway,
just off to a lecture on Beowulf.

Suddenly a rushing of wings
as the generations between accelerate
like a fan of pages riffling over
or like the frames that rattled past
as I swooped into the anaesthetic
for my tonsillectomy, when I was nine.
Face after face, all with our imprint,
humming forwards. We can do anything.

Outside The Crematorium

Flirting with death, after my third funeral
in a month, I chat with the undertaker,
a dashing figure in his designer beard
and frock-coat. He was at school with my son.

They used to play in his father's workshop.
"One day I'll come here in my coffin",
I tell him. "I'd like you to see me off.
Andrew will arrange it. How's the family?"

The last stragglers have viewed the flowers
and are drifting towards their cars. The vicar
has apologised to me for the "poem"
he read with such professional gravity.

Some of my neighbours are walking home –
Peggy was local (the pet-shop lady).
The sun is shining calmly. I could almost
get used to this death business except

that our last funeral was for a baby,
whose grandmother has just been telling us
how she helped to wash and dress her for it,
and how hard it was to get her vest on.

NEWS FROM THE BEAT

I used to wonder whether "beat poet" was the name of a poet who wrote beat poetry, or simply an instruction to "Beat Poet". Suppose it depends which poet you're talking about. I received an email the other day from some people who wanted to do the latter. The subject line read:

"STOLEN FROM THE POOR AND GIVEN TO RICH POETS"

Intrigued, I opened the email.

"You may know the date of World Poetry Day, but you may not know that this day was established by UNESCO as World POVERTY Day."

Gadzooks! Could it be true?

"Poets will have you believe a UNESCO intern simply forgot "V" out of poverty resulting in the abomination that is world POETRY day. But we know that it was stolen. The V was stolen! We want our V back"

The email ended with the usual:

"sign here and send on to fifteen people or you will get writer's block".

Politics is almost as defensive as a dysfunctional writers' workshop. Maybe I should forward the mail to Tony Harrison – for it is he what wrote V. Nah. Always one to be drawn in by a good conspiracy theory I pressed delete and solved the problem. Note to self, "delete more often".

I've just returned from celebrating aforementioned World Poetry Day at the only country in the world with the word "love" in its name. Slovenia. On the night of my arrival I was treated to a sumptuous meal in a restaurant situated above the Writers Association of Slovenia. It's all very Earls Court Poetry Society.

As I parted the flesh from the bones of a perfectly cooked trout an intriguing story unfolded. It was *the* literary story to hit Slovenian News in 2006 – and it's about Jackie Kay. The melt in the mouth potatoes were to die for, bit like Jackie Kay.

Gregor Podlogar*, a Slovenian poet/ broadcaster, handsome and intense, told me of her visit, "she is fantastic", he enthused. The rest of the literary table nodded in agreement. "But I am ashamed", he said, furrowing the brow. The rest of the table shook their heads in solemn agreement. "On her wonderful tour, and only one hour before a prescheduled visit to a Slovenian

Catholic school, the head of the school slammed the door in her face." Gregor was angry and slammed his fist on the table sending bones of trout flying into the air. Masterfully he caught the trout by head and tail and delicately placed the fish skeleton back onto my plate. He emphasised and growled each grave word, "It. Was. A. Disgrrrrrace".

No, the trout was wonderful, really. See, the Catholic school thought Jackie Kay "A Friend of Dorothy". Jackie Kay had unwittingly touched a nerve, by being born. It became national news and the Slovenian press defended Ms Kay. I am delighted to inform *PR* that Ms Kay's book sales elegantly rose to the occasion and by that simple and triumphant action the fist of poetic justice punched the teeth out of institutional bigotry. Thwack. Duff! Zap. Now there's a royalty statement if ever there was one! Biff!

The population of Slovenia is an eighth of that of London and it's the first of the post-Yugoslavian countries to join the EU. In one day I do three readings, two television interviews and one radio interview – that's the population covered then.

Back in a more sedate England I'm on another plane to another country, Sweden, and another venue, Gothenburg's World Museum of Culture. But technology is persistent and, like a flash, BBC Radio Four have booked a studio in Gothenburg for a programme called *Word Of Mouth*. There's a simile competition back in the UK and I'm a judge. Being a judge of a simile competition is rather like being an accountant in *Alice in Wonderland* – a bit discombobulating.

On the way to the studio, hurrying through snow-lined streets in a taxi, I'm reading *Bravemouth* by Pamela Stevenson. She says of her globetrotting husband Billy Connolly, "he is as close to me as tears". Now there's a simile. The taxi driver is built like Hagrid from the Harry Potter novels. He seems to fill the entire front of the Mercedes. He writes himself and I find myself embroiled in a discussion about metaphor and simile. "Metaphor metaphor," he blurts, "that's a load of rubbish". He winks in the mirror.

LEMN SISSAY

* see also poem by Tomaž Šalamun, pp. 31-2

DAME MURIEL SPARK
1918–2006

Dame Muriel Spark, the satirical post-war novelist and a former editor of *Poetry Review*, died in April aged eighty-eight. Born Muriel Camberg in 1918, the reclusive Scottish writer had been living in Italy since 1968.

Author of more than twenty novels, all written in longhand, Muriel Spark's first literary efforts were poetic; aged just fourteen, she won the Walter Scott Prize for Poetry, later saying, "I have always thought of myself as a poet. I do not write poetic prose, but feel that my outlook on life and perceptions of events are those of a poet." Co-author of various critical studies, she also wrote anti-Nazi propaganda for MI5 during the war, once telling the Germans that Hitler's trousers had been burnt off.

It was not until 1957, by then a divorced single mother of thirty-nine, that Muriel Spark published her first novel, *The Comforters*. A recent convert to Catholicism, Spark's dark mordant wit was to become her trademark as a novelist, most notably in *The Prime of Miss Jean Brodie*, whose extravagant heroine was partly inspired by Christina Kay, one of her own teachers at the James Gillespie School in her native Edinburgh.

Muriel Spark was a staunch champion of modernism, admiring poets like T. S. Eliot and Ezra Pound. Though her editorship of *Poetry Review* ended in controversy after less than two years, she said in 2005, "I think it wonderful that a woman editor is taking over again and I hope she will be as successful in attracting good poetry to the Society as I believe I was, a way back in 1947."

A new paperback edition of Muriel Spark's collected poems, *All the Poems* has just been published (Carcanet, £9.95, ISBN 1857548906).

JANE HOLLAND

LETTER TO THE EDITOR

I've decided, reluctantly, to self publish my second collection of children's poems. Despite the comparative success of my first self published collection (shortlisted for the inaugural CLPE Poetry Award, stocked by Ottakars, Waterstone's etc.), mainstream publishers are still disinclined to take on single author collections.

The state of children's poetry publishing concerns me greatly. How are children to become familiar with a body of work by poets, and thereby cultivate an interest which will carry them through to adulthood? There aren't any prizes specifically for new single author collections (the CLPE Award has been won by anthologies, or a 'selected poems' so far), which doesn't compare at all with children's fiction. When I visit primary schools, children can rarely name any poets [...]

CHRISSIE GITTINS, FOREST HILL, LONDON

James Harpur
A Martian Sends An E-Mail Home

Poets make dainty patterns known as poems
by feeding paper through a plastic box

but need an expert called a *feckingcritic*
to say if they are beautiful or not.

A reading's when a poet stands on trial
to confess to crimes of passion (I think):

a jury claps to stop the pain, retires,
but does not reconvene to give a verdict.

Magazines are clever: they send you poems
identical to ones that you have written

enclosed in envelopes addressed to you
in handwriting exactly like your own.

Competitions are a service for unwanted poems –
you simply send them off with sums of money;

sometimes, if poems cannot be disposed of
you get some money back as compensation.

Collections are creatures with sticky spines
who catch old poems for their food;

nocturnal, they rarely see the light of day –
unless they have been bred on Planet Ulster.

Publishers are almost always out to lunch.
They stare at televisions known as screens

and receive a lot of poems entitled 'Pay'
which they deposit in a library called a bank.

CONTRIBUTORS

Moniza Alvi's latest collection is *How The Stone Found Its Voice* (Bloodaxe, 2005). See Ruth Padel's reading on pp.87–8

Tiffany Atkinson's *Kink And Particle* is published by Seren in the autumn.

John Burnside's *Selected Poems* and a memoir, *A Lie About My Father*, both published by Cape this year, are reviewed on pp. 101–104.

Elaine Feinstein's *Collected Poems and Translations* (2002) was a PBS Special Commendation.

Philip Gross's latest collection is *The Egg of Zero* (Bloodaxe, 2006). His *Mappa Mundi* (2003) was a PBS Recommendation.

James Harpur's collections of poetry include *Oracle Bones* (Anvil, 2003).

Jane Holland's *The Brief History of a Disreputable Woman* was published by Bloodaxe in 1997. She edits *Poets on Fire* (poetsonfire.blogspot.com)

Lucien Jenkins is a musicologist whose first collection, *Laying Out The Body*, was published by Seren in 1992.

Lotte Kramer, who arrived in Britain on a Kindertransport in 1939, has published ten collections, most recently *Black Over Red* (2005, Rockingham).

Bill Manhire, the inaugural New Zealand Poet Laureate, has won the New Zealand Book Award for Poetry five times. His *Collected Poems* was published in 2001.

W. S. Merwin's new and selected poems, *Migration*, won the 2005 National Book Award for Poetry.

Andrew Motion's memoir of childhood, *In the Blood*, is published by Faber in the autumn.

Daljit Nagra's poem 'Look We Have Coming To Dover!' won the 2005 Forward Prize. Faber will publish his first collection in 2007.

Ruth Padel's *Voodoo Shop* was shortlisted for the 2002 T. S. Eliot and Whitbread Prizes; her *The Soho Leopard* (2004) was a PBS Choice.

Don Paterson's *Landing Light* won the 2003 T. S. Eliot Prize and the 2003 Whitbread Poetry Award. His version of Rilke's *Sonnets to Orpheus* is published in October.

Jacob Polley's first collection, *The Brink* (Picador, 2003), was selected for the Next Generation promotion.

Tracy Ryan's *Hothouse* appears later this year from Arc. She lives and works in Australia.

Tomaž Šalamun's latest books in English are *The Book For My Brother* (Harcourt, 2005) and *Row* (Arc, 2005).

Michael Schmidt is Professor of Poetry at the University of Glasgow, editorial and managing director of Carcanet Press, and editor of *PN Review*.

Subscribe to POETRY REVIEW
the UK's oldest and most widely read poetry magazine

Four issues including postage   UK: £30 inc p&p   Overseas: £40 inc p&p
Please contact us on 020 7420 9881 for insitutional rates

☐ I enclose a cheque for £_____   **OR** ☐ Please debit £ _____ from my card

Title _____   First Name _____   Surname _____

House no. ____   Address _____

_____   Postcode _____

Telephone _____   Email _____

Card details (Visa/Switch/Mastercard/Solo)   Issue number (Switch only) ☐☐

Cardholder's name _____

Card number ☐☐☐☐ ☐☐☐☐ ☐☐☐☐ ☐☐☐☐ ☐☐☐
(please note, if paying by Switch, the card number is the long number above your name)

Security code ☐☐☐☐   Expiry date ☐☐☐☐   Valid from date ☐☐☐☐
(This is the 3 or 4 digit number which forms the last block of numbers on the signature strip on the back)

Signature _____   Date _____

POETRY REVIEW – Gift Subscription

Four issues including postage   UK: £30 inc p&p   Overseas: £40 inc p&p

☐ I enclose a cheque for £_____   **OR** ☐ Please debit £ _____ from my card

Title _____   First Name _____   Surname _____

House no. ____   Address _____

_____   Postcode _____   Telephone _____

Card details (Visa/Switch/Mastercard/Solo)   Issue number (Switch only) ☐☐
(delete as appropriate)

Cardholder's name _____

Card number ☐☐☐☐ ☐☐☐☐ ☐☐☐☐ ☐☐☐☐ ☐☐☐
(please note, if paying by Switch, the card number is the long number above your name)

Security code ☐☐☐☐   Expiry date ☐☐☐☐   Valid from date ☐☐☐☐
(This is the 3 or 4 digit number which forms the last block of numbers on the signature strip on the back)

Signature _____   Date _____

Please send the gift subscription to:

Title _____   First Name _____   Surname _____

House no. ____   Address _____

_____   Postcode _____

Please fold here and tape or staple closed

Please affix stamp if posting from outside UK

Poetry Review Subscriptions
FREEPOST LON5410
London WC2H 9BR

Please fold here and tape or staple closed